Resting in Him
FINDING PEACE IN THE UNEXPECTED

Resting in Him
FINDING PEACE IN THE UNEXPECTED

APRIL L. GAMMON
NASHVILLE, TENNESSEE

Copyright © 2018 by April Gammon
Illustration © 2018 by Faith Fonfara
Editing and design by thecreativeperch.com
All rights reserved.

Scripture quotations marked NKJV taken from the New King James Version®. Copyright © 1982 by Thomas Nelson. Used by permission. All rights reserved.

Scripture quotations marked NASB taken from the New American Standard Bible®. Copyright © 1960, 1962, 1963, 1968, 1971, 1972, 1973, 1975, 1977, 1995 by The Lockman Foundation. Used by permission. www.Lockman.org

Scripture quotations marked GW are taken from GOD'S WORD®, © 1995 by God's Word to the Nations. Used by permission of Baker Publishing Group.

Scripture quotations marked AMPC are taken from the Amplified® Bible, Copyright © 1954, 1958, 1962, 1964, 1965, 1987 by The Lockman Foundation. Used by permission. www.Lockman.org

Scripture quotations marked NIV are taken from the Holy Bible, New International Version®, NIV®. Copyright © 1973, 1978, 1984, 2011 by Biblica, Inc™. Used by permission of Zondervan. All rights reserved worldwide. www.zondervan.com. The "NIV" and "New International Version" are trademarks registered in the United States Patent and Trademark Office by Biblica, Inc™.

Scripture quotations marked ESV are taken from The Holy Bible, English Standard Version®. Copyright © 2001 by Crossway, a publishing ministry of Good News Publishers. Used by permission. All rights reserved.

Scripture quotations marked HCSB® are taken from the Holman Christian Standard Bible®. Copyright © 1999, 2000, 2002, 2003, 2009 by Holman Bible Publishers. Used by permission. HCSB® is a federally registered trademark of Holman Bible Publishers.

Scripture quotations marked KJ2000 are taken from King James 2000 Bible, Copyright © Dr. Robert A. Couric, ThD, Editor, 2000, 2003. Used by permission.

Scripture quotations marked NRSV taken from New Revised Standard Version Bible, copyright ©1989, National Council of the Churches of Christ in the United States of America. Used by permission.

Scripture quotations marked NLT are taken from the Holy Bible, New Living Translation, copyright © 1996, 2004, 2015 by Tyndale House Foundation. Used by permission of Tyndale House Publishers, Inc., Carol Stream, IL 60188. All rights reserved.

Scripture quotations marked NET are taken from the NET Bible®, Copyright © 1996–2017 by Biblical Studies Press, LLC. http://Netbible.com. All rights reserved. Used by permission of Biblical Studies Press, Richardson, TX.

Scripture quotations marked NCV are taken from the New Century Version®. Copyright © 2005 by Thomas Nelson. Used by permission. All rights reserved.

All other scripture quotations are from the King James Version.

Epigraph

*"It's hard to believe how much
I love him so deeply, so unconditionally,
just deep down in the core of my being," I said.*

*Then God spoke softly to my heart,
"That's how I love you, but more!"*

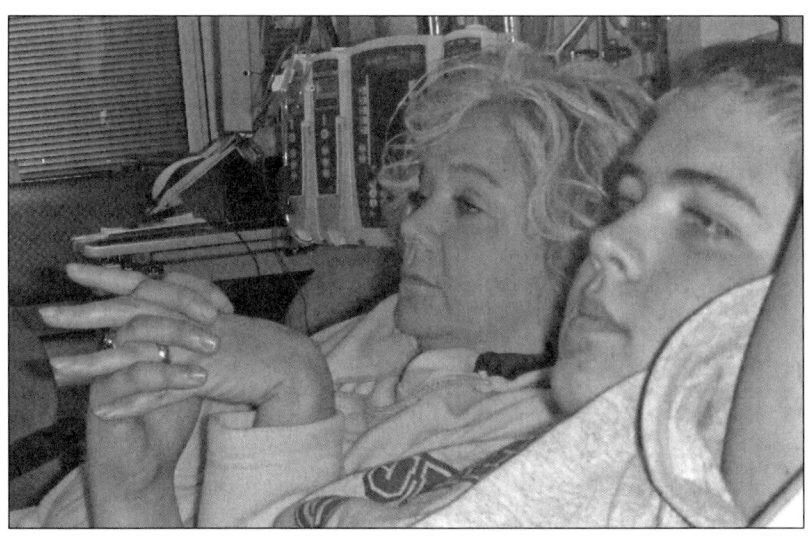

Dedication

In loving memory of my oldest son, Dustan Gammon.

I love you and miss you more than words could ever describe. You were my inspiration for this book. A promise kept. Your strength, determination, faith, and all-out fight for life pushed me in my darkest moments of writing. The memory of your sweet face and beautiful smile kept me moving forward. Your pure, unwavering love for Jesus inspired me to find my own healing in the arms of the One who welcomed you home. I believe your legacy of faith and love will continue for generations to come.

I dedicate this book, our own story to

Dylan

You are my precious "baby-man". You are my laughter in the still moments of life. You have traveled a road no one asks for, and yet, you paved your own way through the grief journey. You inspire me to be a better writer, speaker, and lover of Jesus. Your gentle nudges of encouragement have kept my feet on the tough road of writing. Your "Big Dream" mentality has encouraged me to go places I never imagined possible. I love you and am so proud of the dreamer you are!

Kenny

To my best friend. The one who stands beside me to encourage, behind me to support, in front of me to lead. You are my voice of reason when life is chaotic. You believe in me more than I do myself. Thank you for being my biggest fan and cheerleader. You are patient, kind, gentle, loving, and you always see the bright side of every situation. You keep my feet planted, my head focused, and my heart tender. For you I prayed and God was faithful in giving me my heart's desire. A man after his own heart. Our road has not always been easy, but we have laughed, cried, crawled, walked, and run together. You have been my faithful companion on this journey and I would never want to live this life without you. Love you BIG!

Contents

Biography .... *viii*

Foreword by Jennifer Christensen x

Preface, *"Dear Reader"* .... *xii*

1	*Preparation for the Journey* 1
2	*Our Journey Begins* 9
3	*Broken Dreams* 33
4	*Rope of Hope* 51
5	*Brotherly Love* 69
6	*Miracles Seen and Unseen* 89
7	*What Was, What Is, What Will Be* 105
8	*Taking a Step Out of the Boat* 119
9	*The Ultimate Sacrifice* 131
10	*The Healing Process* 145
11	*Treasures I Found in the Dark* 161
12	*It's a God Thing* 177
13	*The Number Thirty-One* 193

Conclusion, *Those Who Sow in Tears Shall Reap in Joy* 207

Bibliography 211

Eulogy *213*

Biography

Dustan Gammon was born on May 7, 1990, in Nashville, Tennessee. He attended Metro Christian Academy from kindergarten to eighth grade. While there he excelled in basketball and soccer. He played the trumpet in the school band and won several Christian vocal awards.

One day when he was about twelve years old he decided he wanted to play the drums; so he sat down, with drumsticks in hand, and began to play. No lessons needed. He had a natural beat that no one else could follow. From that day on, he started playing drums for the praise and worship team at Family Worship Center.

The beginning of his ninth grade year, we moved to Mt. Juliet and he enrolled in Mt. Juliet Christian Academy. He joined the marching band, where he played trumpet and French horn. He was also actively involved on the baseball and basketball teams.

In October 2005, during his sophomore year, he was diagnosed with acute lymphatic leukemia. He was devastated. But he decided not to ask, "Why me?" He was going to fight this battle head on, with courage and strength. That he did.

He went into remission within six weeks and spent most of his sophomore year in Vanderbilt Children's hospital facing chemotherapy treatments. He worked very hard to keep up his schoolwork and to continue being a part of the basketball and baseball teams and playing drums in the praise and worship band. He also was the assistant coach of his high school basketball team.

After twelve months, October 2006, his junior year, he relapsed. He started more aggressive treatments. Then in October 2007, his senior year, he relapsed a third time. Now his only option was a bone marrow transplant.

During his senior year in high school he was faced with harsh chemotherapy and radiation treatments that made him very ill. Nevertheless, he was determined to walk with his senior class. He worked hard to keep up his schoolwork and still be a part of his senior class. He showed an enormous amount of faith and courage throughout his constant battles with cancer. He brought his school and fellow students to a new level of brotherhood. He exemplified inner strength that showed each one of us that with great determination and faith in God, all things are possible.

In May 2008, he once again relapsed. Determined to walk with his senior class, he decided to put his treatments on hold.
May 7, 2008, Dustan turned eighteen years old.
May 30, 2008, Dustan graduated with his class from Mt. Juliet Christian Academy.
June 28, 2008, Dustan graduated to eternal life.

Foreword

I think it's his eyes I remember most, equal parts wisdom and mischief. No matter what happened to his body, his face, his hair…his eyes always stayed the same. I was Dustan Gammon's high school English teacher by assignment. Dustan was my teacher by providence.

The senior year has always been my favorite to teach. There is just something special about wrapping up a journey that began before those students could tie their own shoes. So, that early August morning when Dustan crossed my classroom threshold was infused with both anticipation and hope. I knew him as the young man who had taken on cancer and won. Remission. Reprieve. Since his sophomore year, he had worked through obstacles that most of my students would never understand. He had shouldered unimaginable pain. He had already walked through the valley of the shadow of death and had crossed through to the other side. Dustan was still dealing with the effects of that battle, however. I remember distinctly how his hair was growing back and filling in. He ran his hand over the top of his skull with a sheepish grin. Finally, this was going to be a good year.

I had students do typical first day senior assignments. One was a letter they wrote to themselves about the year ahead. The prompt was simple: "What is one thing you are looking forward to? What is one thing you fear?" I asked students to share their responses. Sitting in the front row, right corner, Dustan spoke freely, "I'm excited about graduating. I'm afraid my cancer will come back."

It did. That fall it returned, and once again he fell into the cycle of sickness. Time passed as he anticipated a bone marrow transplant, the antidote to death. His brave brother, Dylan, was a match, and the school turned its head once again toward hope. We sold t-shirts in his favorite color. We campaigned for his healing. We prayed and cried and pleaded.

I started bringing Dustan his make-up work after he was healthy enough to receive visitors. His mission was clear: graduation. As I left healthy, able-bodied seniors each day at school who could barely stay awake, I would drive to Dustan, recuperating relentlessly. His work ethic was punishing. He was going to walk across that stage, grab that diploma, and live the life he had dreamed. Of that, he was certain.

And then, just as swiftly as it had receded, the evil one returned one last time, just weeks before graduation. Dustan, with his original goal in mind, kept working toward that special night. To this day, in my career, the longest sustained ovation of applause I have ever heard was reserved for Dustan, as he strode confidently across the finish line, turning his tassel with all of his other classmates.

I still don't know why God chose to cross our paths. There were more worthy recipients for Dustan's influence, for certain. Every year, I still tell his story. I show his picture. There is not a class of students I have taught since his death that leave my room without meeting him. Those pearls of wisdom he left behind still shine. His life still preaches. It matters that he was here. It matters that we are here. Thank you for all you taught me, Dustan…my forever friend.

Jennifer Christensen
Mt. Juliet, Tennessee, 2018

Preface

Dear Reader,

You are about to embark on a heart-wrenching, heart-warming, heart-changing journey. As you travel through the years of our eldest son's cancer, his untimely death, our family's grief, and the healing process, you will more than likely succumb to many emotions. Grab a box of tissues. Maybe even a box of chocolates. For me, the author, I had to revisit many places of my heart that still were a little raw and had not completely healed. So I needed both!

I wrote this book for our family as a testimony to God's purpose and presence in the many seasons of our lives. I wrote this book for you, dear reader, so that you may also look back and see the handprints of God in your own life. Our stories may be somewhat different, but there will always be a common thread throughout; we will all experience pain, loss, brokenness, and powerlessness.

As you read the following pages you will see the progression of our family's discovery of our heavenly Father's true unconditional love and grace. Our family lived inside a God-shaped box that had rules, regulations, and religion. You will witness as you read some of my own personal journaling how God slowly and meticulously took me from a checklist, rule-following Christian to a carefree, grace-filled daughter.

Our family, especially me, needed balance in our lives. We knew we served a God who heals, delivers, and blesses His children. Oh, we had faith in God—but had lost the ability to see and feel His love for us. We had gotten comfortable with our Christianity and had forgotten the most important part, which was our relationship with Christ.

I encourage you as you read the pages of our story: keep your heart open so that you will truly see that this is God's story. It is where He took a very difficult season of our lives and sprinkled it with His love and grace. Now our story, told by me, but written by God, is filled with purpose, life, wholeness, and JOY!

God is a good God and wants only good for His children. Circumstances do not change His goodness. My unanswered questions do not change His goodness. I have learned by walking a very difficult road that our God is *not* a cancer-causing Creator. He is a loving, life-giving Lord.

I pray as you turn each page you sense God's love for you. If there is anything I want you as the reader to take from this book, it is that God loves you. He is waiting and He is willing to be all that you need Him to be.

And maybe you are in a season in which He is all that you have. Oh, reader, what better place could there be but right there with Him?

Resting!

April Gammon

April Gammon

CHAPTER 1

Preparation for the Journey

And God saw everything that he had made, and, behold, it was very good.
(GENESIS 1:31, ASV)

Dear God, Are you there? It's April...

I am sitting in the hospital room with Dustan. I assume you know that already. I really can't talk with anyone, especially Dustan. I am really tired and very frustrated.

You know that I trust you because you are all I have. I don't understand why this is happening and I am trying hard not to question why. This is really hard. Dustan is a really good boy trying to do all the right things. Is this an attack from satan or something we caused? You know the questions are there. I try not to ask anything out loud; then it doesn't seem as bad. My heart aches terribly.

RESTING IN HIM

Everyone says, Oh, you are so strong. What does that mean...strong? I do not feel strong. Really, I don't feel anything. Is that true? NO... I feel guilt, because I can't do anything for Dustan, I am not there for Dylan, and cannot comfort Kenny. What kind of mother, wife or person am I? Tears, tears, tears....

This was one of many entries in my journal. Dustan had already been diagnosed with acute lymphatic leukemia (ALL) and had been in treatment for about four months when I decided to write down some thoughts.

There are no words to describe how you feel when your child receives the news that he has cancer. This is our story; a story of how a young teenage boy faces the devastating news that he has cancer, and how God transforms this boy into a man of faith. Also, how our family continues to be transformed day by day—because of his walk of faith.

It all started on a normal fall day. I use the word "normal" because, as you will find in our story, normal becomes something of an enigma to us. Our eldest son, Dustan Noble Gammon, was diagnosed with ALL on October 5, 2005, at the age of fifteen, just when most teenagers are starting their normal high school years. Dustan was starting his sophomore year and excited about the marching band, basketball, and all that the next three years held for him.

The day we received the phone call from our doctor's office that we needed to go to the emergency room immediately was the day our new journey began. Our journey, I call it, but in reality it would become our new normal. Normal is such a funny word to me now. You see, if you had asked me if we were a normal family, I would have said, Of course. Two working parents, two sons, building a new house, and very active in our church, a middle class family is how I would have described us.

Perfect, no; but happy. Until, we heard the word *cancer*.

Preparation for the Journey

The scene burned into my memory. Our family is gathered around Dustan's bed. The doctors come in and say, We are sorry to tell you but our tests have confirmed your son does have leukemia. I am sitting by Dustan and his head drops to my shoulder with tears running down his face.

I grabbed his face in my hand, looked him in the eyes, and said, "Everything will be fine, we will beat this."

He wiped the tears from his eyes, looked at the doctors, and said, "Tell me what I have to do to make this cancer go away."

Little did I know—from that moment my son was going to show *me* the strength and faith that it would take to battle this horrible disease.

Looking back now I can see how our heavenly Father was already preparing us for a journey we neither chose nor wanted to walk. Kenny (my husband), Dylan (our youngest son), Dustan, and I were thrown into our new normal. Doctor visits, hospital stays, chemotherapy, medicines, surgeries, tests, and the list goes on and on. Our new normal.

Preparation for our journey started the day Dustan was born! I can see now God was grooming him to be a very unique, talented, strong young man. Dustan was six years old when he accepted Christ as his personal Savior. The night he was baptized he sang a special, the song "God is still working on me." He had a very angelic voice; and he used his voice.

He sang at church and at school. In school he won several awards both for his singing and trumpet playing. God had gifted him and he was using his gift for God's glory even at a very young age. At the age of twelve he decided he wanted to play the drums at our church. He sat down one day, picked up the drumsticks, and started playing to a beat all his own. The drums became his passion; that is literally what got him through many difficult times as he underwent cancer treatments. No matter how he felt he played the drums with a passion and a purpose. It was just him, the drums, his music, and God.

Playing the drums is also what became his and his dad's connection. Kenny was our praise and worship leader and Dustan played for him. The bond they had with their music was like no other. I am convinced that God knew this is what would get Dustan through these difficult years.

God was also preparing the rest of our family. Just a year prior to Dustan's diagnosis God had led us to a new Christian school, Mt. Juliet Christian Academy, after being at another Christian school for nine years. God had placed us there because He knew what was ahead for us. You will see in the later chapters how the students, parents, and the faculty played an intricate part in our journey.

That was also the year God shared with me in my quiet time that I would start learning to be a prayer warrior—that I needed to be ready to face some spiritual battles, and to start getting in His word and put the full armor on for the battle that was ahead.

Isn't it just like God to prepare us? He loves us so much He wants us to be prepared. We as Christians need to learn to hear the voice of God and be obedient to His leading. He wants what is best for us. He is always looking out for our good even when it can be painful.

When I started thinking about putting on the whole armor of God, I thought this meant I just needed to read His word and be faithful in my Christian works.

No, that is not it at all. Putting on the whole armor of God means getting dressed from head to toe in His word. Ephesians 6:14–17 (NKJV), "Stand therefore, having girded your waist with truth, having put on the breastplate of righteousness, and having shod your feet with the preparation of the gospel of peace; above all, taking the shield of faith with which you will be able to quench all the fiery darts of the

Preparation for the Journey

wicked one. And take the helmet of salvation, and the sword of the Spirit, which is the word of God." God was preparing us for a battle. I was learning a little at a time that taking on the whole armor of God would be a constant in my life. It was not going to be easy, but we sure were going to try. We wanted to win this battle.

Just one month prior to the diagnosis, Kenny and I felt God's leading to do a Daniel fast. The Daniel fast is a fast from certain foods for health and healing. As Job said, "I have not departed from the commandment of His lips; I have treasured the words of His mouth more than my necessary food" (Job 23:12, NKJV). Not knowing the full meaning of our fast, we just wanted to be obedient to God's leading. That was very important to us. This was the first time we had ever done a fast for twenty-one days. I knew God would bless our obedience and give us insight that would be needed.

This fast not only prepared me but changed me. I was taking additional time in God's word, and He was revealing His truth to me little by little. Not until October 5, 2005, would this truth be revealed as our only hope in a desperate situation.

Daniel 1:8 states, "But Daniel purposed in his heart." Daniel was not going to let his difficult circumstances define his future. Even with all he was facing it would not hinder the plan of God for his life. Daniel did not let his captivity take his hopes and dreams, and neither were we. God was preparing us for the unseen circumstances ahead. We just had to have the faith in God that He would not fail us.

At the time of the fast we were in the process of building a new house for ourselves. We had also just completed building a house to sell. We were thinking we were fasting for direction and wisdom for these two houses. It was not until later we realized our fast was preparing us for our new journey—Dustan's life.

God allows us only small nuggets of revelation at a time. He knows exactly what we need to know and when we need to know it. Still, we are earthly beings, living in a fleshly body, our "earth suits," as I have heard it called; and our minds are set on the flesh. So we usually try to make a new nugget of revelation fit into what we already think.

> *For those who live according to the flesh*
> *set their minds on the things of the flesh,*
> *but those who live according to the Spirit,*
> *the things of the Spirit.*
> (ROMANS 8:5, NASB)

It may be sometime later we realize that God's reason for revealing this new thing to us wasn't what we first thought. As He trains our minds to become Spirit-led, then we see its true meaning.

Have you ever thought the things that happen in your life are just random events? "Your eyes saw my substance, being yet unformed. And in Your book they all were written, the days fashioned for me, When as yet there were none of them" (Psalm 139:16, NKJV). God loves us so unconditionally He gives us our free will. Whether we choose to walk in His path (*Spirit*) or our path (*flesh*), He will cause all things to work together for our good.

Our prayer in the very beginning of this journey was, "You are the Lord of our lives and you knew before this day arrived what would occur. You have seen all our ways prior to this day, and you already knew how we would respond. Now lead us in your wisdom and your strength through this new journey. Guide us along this road of uncertainty, give us your peace that surpasses **all** understanding. We know that you are a God that heals, that provides all that we need; and we put ALL our trust in you."

Once we prayed this and believed this with everything we had in us we began to stand on His word. Were there doubts? No! Were there occasions for us to

Preparation for the Journey

get weary and downhearted? Yes! God was faithful in giving us that peace that surpasses all understanding. Philippians 6:6,7 (NKJV), "Be anxious for nothing, but in everything by prayer and supplication, with thanksgiving, let your requests be made known to God; and the peace of God, which surpasses all understanding, will guard your hearts and minds through Christ Jesus."

Everything in our lives prior to the date of Dustan's diagnosis had prepared us for this day. Were we ready for this part of our journey? Honestly, I do not think you can ever be prepared to go through what my precious son was about to embark upon. Spiritually God was already preparing us, but physically and emotionally we were dangling over a cliff of the unknown.

Even today God still reveals to me how He was preparing us prior to Dustan's diagnosis. As you continue to grow in your relationship with Christ He will continue to reveal your own personal nuggets to you. Oh, how I have learned to cherish these nuggets. The more God knows that you are prepared, the more He will reveal. This has become one of my treasures in my relationship with Christ. You see, as He gives me my own personal nugget I know He is preparing me for the next step in my journey of life. It will only be something that is for my own good. When His timing is perfect He will then reveal His glorious light, so that I can see the truth of my nugget.

The chapters ahead invite you to walk our journey with us. You will see how God led a normal (remember, *normal* is still a mystery to us) family along an unimaginable path, and transformed a fifteen-year-old boy into a man of faith. And Dustan's faith continues bearing fruit, as God has continued transforming our family.

CHAPTER 2

Our Journey Begins

*I know the plans that I have for you, declares the Lord.
They are plans for peace and not disaster,
plans to give you a future filled with hope.*
(JEREMIAH 29:11, GW)

Lord, where do I begin? We are now halfway through this. [I thought.] *Sometimes it seems I am going under, but you are taking me over. I watch my son in such pain and I realize you are bigger than this. I feel just a little of what you must feel when your children are in agony and pain. It hurts so deep within. Lord, forgive my unbelief. I know all things are for your purpose. My trust is in you, Lord—in you! In you! You have taken us through the hard times and you will continue to do so. To every thing there is a season, a time to every purpose under the heaven, Ecclesiastes 3:1. What else do I have to hope in but you, Lord?*

RESTING IN HIM

I ask Lord that you renew the spirit of faith in me that is so strong that it shines through me to my whole family. That they see your love and your faithfulness. Be not afraid, only believe, Mark 5:36.

I have decided that I am just a passenger on this ride. Jesus is in the driver's seat, and so our journey begins....

Have you ever gone to an amusement park with overwhelming anticipation of the fun and excitement that awaited you there? Despite your awareness that too much food plus exciting rides would bring on that queasy feeling in the pit of your stomach, you knew it would all be worth it. You did not care because you would be having the time of your life.

This describes our journey. We were anticipating fun and excitement for our sons in their high school years. Kenny and I had often thought about that time in the future with such joy. We had such high hopes. We knew the teenage years would not be easy, but we were ready to face all that was ahead of us. All, of course, except cancer. That was nothing we had dreamed nor envisioned for either of our sons. It did not matter now. Cancer was here, and we had to face it head on.

All our excitement came to a halt on that dreadful October day. All our hopes and dreams came crashing down. All I knew was my son was sick, lying in a hospital bed, and he needed to know everything was going to be okay. He needed to know that the God we said we served was going to come through for him. He needed to feel God's peace and comfort like he had never known before. Most fifteen-year-olds do not have to trust God for their life. Dustan did.

Cancer does not affect just the one who has it, but touches each person in the family. All our lives as we knew them would change. Dustan would have to face his fears. Dylan would have to adjust to his new role in the family. Kenny would have to relinquish his right of fatherly protection. As for me, I would have to learn to trust that my heavenly Father loves my son even more than I do. That was difficult to learn as I watched my son suffer both emotionally and physically every day.

As I said previously, our journey with cancer would leave us with a queasy feeling in the pit of our stomachs. Our excitement about the future turned into fear. Dustan had never been sick, other than your normal childhood illnesses. Now, we were faced with this horrible disease and we were not sure of anything any more. All I could think of was that someone had to make my son better and NOW.

As a mother, how do you sit back and watch your son suffer day in and day out? With arms tied, the helplessness became overwhelming. I just wanted to take him in my arms and protect him. My insides were screaming NO! NO! Yet, I had to be calm for Dustan and the rest of our family. I had to come to a realization that this was our reality and decide quickly how to deal with what was happening. I was a Christian, so I assumed the best thing to do was to trust God. I did not realize all that would entail.

Being a Christian and trusting God had been pretty easy my whole life, until now. This was a crossroads: whether I was going to believe what I had always been taught, or crumble in unbelief. I chose to trust God. It amazes me how we turn to God and trust Him pretty quickly when He becomes all we have.

At this point, although we were trusting in God, we still had to follow the doctors' advice. Truthfully, they dealt with this on a daily basis, and if they didn't know how to handle this, who did? So we decided to put confidence in the doctors, but we reserved our trust for God alone.

We had walked through the first two years of our cancer journey with high expectations regarding the prognosis issued by man. Dustan was given a 94% recovery rate even though he was considered a high risk because of his age. Most

RESTING IN HIM

childhood leukemia patients are under the age of twelve. We were confident that the doctors knew the best plan for recovery. So we continued with the roadmap set out before him by his doctors, and we knew with everything inside us Dustan was going to be fine. God had given us peace from the very beginning; and still we had to trust the doctors, while Dustan had to go through all the treatments. We were excited because we knew even though this was going to be a long, hard battle, it was all going to be worth it when the treatments were over. Dustan was going to be able to go on with his life, go to college, get married, and live out his God-given destiny.

Part of settling into our new normal was embracing the idea of the amusement park. We had no idea what was awaiting us. We knew we had to continue to walk and to do everything that was expected of us medically. Then came the queasy feeling in the pit of my stomach, the pain of watching my precious son undergo such extreme measures to get rid of this cancer.

I am sure there is no comparison to what Jesus went through on the cross, but while sitting by my son's hospital bed one night, God gave me a little insight into what Mary must have felt. These were my thoughts as I wrote in my journal:

Sitting in the hospital listening to Dustan moan and hum as the medicine makes him sleep, my mind goes to Mary, the mother of Jesus. Oh, how I feel her heart. She watched her son be crucified for the world. Crucified so that He may save the world. How my heart aches as I watch my son be crucified by chemo. The reason is unknown but for God to get the glory! I think about Jesus and the Father, and how His heart must ache when He sees Dustan lying there with poison going through his body. But then how His heart leaps for joy when He knows Dustan still knows that He is a good God. He knows Dustan still trusts in Him.

Why must evil happen to good people? We live in an evil world, so we cannot escape the evil that is before us—or even surrounds us. We just have to remember

Our Journey Begins

that God has authority over our destiny, but He still gives us our own free will. If we are His children, I believe God looks at our hearts to see what we truly believe, just as we look at our children. We love our children desperately with everything inside our souls, but if our children continue to be disobedient and walk a life that is not best for them, then they tie our hands. We do the same to our Father. He can step in and use us and guide us, if we give everything over to Him. We must be obedient to His word. Then we can walk in the wonderful path He has for us. Not only can we walk in that path but we can walk hand in hand with our heavenly Father. God's perfect will for us—what an awesome thought!

As I wrote these thoughts, pain, suffering, and evil were brought into a new focus in my life. I had suffered, I had pain, and I dealt with evil. Now I had to step back and watch these things happen to someone I loved so deeply. How do I handle this? How do I watch my son suffer in pain knowing that this is an evil he did not cause?

My hands were tied. Dustan was putting his trust in me and Kenny to make the right decisions for him. Dustan had his free will to say no, but his trust was in us. How do you make these decisions, thinking they are right but knowing they are going to cause your child such pain. You can see the future. You can see the bigger picture. You know what he is suffering through will ultimately be for his betterment. As much as you hate it, you have to stand back and watch. You do so because you love him. Is this how my Father feels? We were trusting Him knowing He could see the future, the big picture. We were trusting through our pain—through Dustan's pain.

There were so many times I had to literally give my son over to my heavenly Father. I would pray: "Okay, Father, Dustan is yours." Then I would take him back and cradle him in my own arms. I knew Dustan had done nothing to cause this cancer. "The thief cometh not, but for to steal, and to kill, and to destroy: I am come that they might have life, and that they might have it more abundantly" (John 10:10). I knew that we served a God who was good and came to give us life, not take it away. I just could not understand why my son had to go through such pain.

RESTING IN HIM

God takes all that is meant for evil and turns it for the good for those who love him. "We are assured and know that [God being a partner in their labor] all things work together and are [fitting into a plan] for good to and for those who love God and are called according to [His] design and purpose" (Romans 8:28, AMPC).

Even though I did not have the answer to my question *Why my son,* I did have the answer to the question *How?* We were going to put all our trust in Him who is good, who is faithful—in Him who came to give us life and give it more abundantly. It was going to be tough, but with God, all things are possible to him who believes. Knowing that, we believed.

So many times as Dustan and I pulled into the parking garage of Vanderbilt Children's Hospital for our weekly or even daily clinic visits, I would look over at him and wonder what must be going through his mind. Is he scared? Does he think, *Why me, Lord?* Or is he thinking, *Enough is enough.* I would not blame him if he thought all those things. Honestly, if he ever thought them, he never voiced them aloud. His decision from the very first day was not to ask why me. *Let's just do it and move forward.* He definitely had to face his fears, and those fears he faced head on.

Since his earliest years, one of Dustan's biggest fears was needles. He would literally make himself sick just thinking he was getting a shot. I remember one incident so vividly. We had taken Dustan and Dylan to the doctor for their annual check-ups, and Dylan had to get his shots. Dustan sat and cried while watching Dylan get his shots. It showed us from a very early age what a compassion and a tender heart he had for others. As you will continue to see, that compassion and tender heart shows up throughout this journey.

The other fear Dustan had to overcome was fear of the unknown. Most of us, though we may not admit it, have this fear. Dustan always liked to know everything that was going to happen. "No surprises," he would say. We cannot know everything that's going to happen to us, but we all like to think that we control our own lives. Dustan was a lot like me when it came to wanting everything just right in his life. Cancer had thrown a wrench in our controlled filled lives. What does the Father say about control? Are we controlled by our flesh or our spirit?

"But I say, walk and live [habitually] in the [Holy] Spirit [responsive to and controlled and guided by the Spirit]; then you will certainly not gratify the cravings and desires of the flesh (of human nature without God)" (Galatians 5:16, AMPC).

I truly thought I was a Christian who lived through His Spirit. I prayed, read my Bible, and was at church every time the doors were open. I lived according to what His word said. I was not perfect, but I was performing like any other Christian. I did all the *right* things—except to give up full control of my life.

It's pretty much impossible to live through His Spirit if you are in control. Hello, that is your flesh. If you had asked me, I was living a Spirit-led life until I was forced to look at the reality of what a Spirit-led life really was: full surrender of your life (flesh). You give up your life (flesh) to live His life (spirit). If anyone gives his life he will surely find *His* life.

"For whoever is bent on saving his [temporal] life [his comfort and security here] shall lose it [eternal life]; and whoever loses his life [his comfort and security here] for My sake shall find it [life everlasting]" (Matthew 16:25, AMPC).

Not only was I having to trust God with my son's life, I was having to learn to trust God with full surrender of my own life. I was giving up my rights of control and learning to surrender all. Now with surrender comes brokenness. What better way to learn surrender and brokenness than traveling through a world of the unknown.

Going from the known to the unknown was something the entire family had to deal with. The question was, were we going to face the unknown with fear and trembling, or were we going to trust God? This was another part of our "normal" we were trying to settle into, the part of the amusement park I did not like.

Remember when you were standing in line to get on one of those thrill rides? The whole time you are in line, you look over at the ride, you watch the people getting off the ride just to see what the expression is on their face. You want just a little glimpse of what is ahead of you. Should I be scared or excited? Then finally you are able to get on. You buckle yourself in and steady yourself, trying not to think about it. The ride takes off with a quick jerk. You are moving forward and you can kind of see what is ahead, and then all of the sudden you start heading skyward. But that's when you discover that you really can't see what's ahead any more; all you can do is rest your head on the seat, move forward, and trust that whoever is in control of the ride knows what they are doing.

This is where we were. We had been buckled into this ride of cancer, the Ugly Monster ride, as I call it, and it had taken off with a tremendous jerk, but we were moving forward.

At first, we could see what was ahead of us. We thought. Then with another quick jerk, we were heading skyward. We no longer could see with our earthly eyes. We had to lower our heads, close our eyes, and rest. We had to trust God, the God who had foreseen our ride on the Ugly Monster. We had to open our spiritual eyes and be guided by Him. We had to trust Him who alone knew a way to make all these things turn out for our good. I call this faith in action.

Of course, we all know that faith is the substance of things hoped for but the evidence of things not seen. Faith in action is when you have to do something with that hope, and evidence of things you cannot see. We could not see the end of the Ugly Monster, but with our spiritual eyes, we could see the hope of our future. We knew God had given us the promise of a future with hope. "For I know the thoughts that I think toward you, says the Lord, thoughts of peace and not of evil, to give you a future and a hope." We had learned whatever God had promised He would deliver. So we rested in Him as we rode upward into the unknown.

God promises that He will give us His peace. As we rest and wait on Him He will speak to us through His word. He is faithful, and His word is true. "The steps of a [good] man are directed *and* established by the Lord when He delights in his way [and He busies Himself with his every step]" (Psalm 37:23, AMPC). I love the idea of a God who "busies Himself." He is constantly busy with not just part, but every step in our lives. So we can rest in Him and be assured that even though He does not always show us His way for the long distance, He will lead us step by step right now.

> *It is only when our hearts are…*
> *actually at rest in God,*
> *in peaceful and self-oblivious adoration,*
> *that we can hope to show His attractiveness to others.*
> —EVELYN UNDERHILL

From the very beginning, even though we all knew we were going to have to adjust our way of thinking and our comfortable lifestyle, we did not do it with ease. Dustan and I were thrown into our part. We had no time to think about anything—we just had to do it. The doctors dictated our path and controlled our days. Kenny and Dylan were a little different. Not that they had a choice, but they had time to think about their new normal. To this day, I am not sure which was worse: not being able to think about it and deal with it, or having to think about it and deal with it constantly.

We have always been a very close family, and cancer just made us that much closer. You realize that as you are traveling this new path the only ones that truly understand are the ones riding along with you. You can see your other family members, friends,

RESTING IN HIM

companions, church members, and the other people in your life standing there cheering you on, but they are not riding the Ugly Monster with you. There are only four seats on this ride, and we are in it together. If one gets close to falling out, we grab ahold and hang on for dear life. We know as a family of four, we need each one to make it through the ride. As a roller-coaster takes dips, twists, and turns, you become comfortable with the knowledge that you are going to be there for the person next to you—there to lean on as you take that quick turn. There to hold you tightly when you have been thrown from your seat. There to hold your hand when you are moving forward, and there to raise your hands together when you are on the downhill. We all knew we needed each other and there was nothing that would come between us, not even cancer. We were in this together for the long haul.

We also knew that even though the four of us were riding this thing out together, most importantly, the Father was helping us maneuver the ride. There were a lot of times we would look around and wonder where He was. We could not see him, but it was at those times He was literally sitting with us or even pushing our cart back on the tracks.

One of those times was when Dustan had a bad reaction to one of his medicines. We had finally made it to the end of one his strongest treatments. Dustan was in his room at home. We had just finished administering one of his medicines through his port. He was feeling nauseous so I left the room to get him a pill. When I returned he was sitting up on the side of his bed looking very pale. I handed him the pill and something to drink. When I turned and left the room, I heard this muffled sound. Not sure where it was coming from, I turned and looked in Dustan's room. He had fallen back on his bed and was trying with all his might to yell, "Mom!"

I rushed into his room screaming at the top of my lungs, "Call 9-1-1 NOW!" By the time I had gotten to Dustan, his eyes were rolling to the back of his head, he was gasping for breath, and his body was curling up. Not knowing what had happened, I was screaming, "No, God! No!"

Our Journey Begins

I thought he was choking on the pill I had just given him so I put my fingers in his mouth to get it out and he clamped down with all his might. I just starting praying with all I had in me, begging God to let him be okay—not to let my son die. It seemed like hours later, but only ten minutes had elapsed when the paramedics arrived. By this time Dustan was coming to and starting to talk. The paramedics were asking him question after question. Kenny, Dylan, and I were standing there in a daze trying to figure out what had just happened.

The paramedics put Dustan in back of the ambulance. I got in the front, and Kenny and Dylan rode in the car behind. As we rode to the hospital, I could hear Dustan and the paramedic in the back talking. The other paramedic was trying to carry on a conversation with me, and all I was thinking was my son had almost died. In my mind I was holding a serious conversation with God. "Now, God, you know I cannot handle if something happens to my son. I cannot go on without him. Now let's make a pact right now. I promise I will do everything you want, but you have to promise you will not let my son die."

I was desperate, and this called for desperate measures: bargaining with God. Who did I think I was that I could bargain with God? Did I think my performance would help me to get in better graces with God? That He would listen to me and do what I wanted? God knew where I was and He knew my heart. He listened to me, knowing that I would have to figure out that the real answer would be me surrendering my son to Him.

I would have to trust that my heavenly Father loved my son more than I did. It would take me a few whirls on that Ugly Monster to figure this out. Many upside and downside turns. Many times holding on to the bars in front of me until my knuckles turned white.

Oh, God was showing me I had to let go of the bars (control). I had to put my hands in His, and trust His ways. It's easy to let go when you are on the straightway of the ride, but when the ride starts jerking you to the right and to the left, you look for something stable to hang on to, and quickly. Most of the time that trust is in ourselves. *I can handle this, even though I cannot control the circumstances; I can control what happens.*

Really? That's what I thought. Little by little, my Father was encouraging me to loosen my grip from the bars. I would throw myself into His word. I found myself searching and searching for those scriptures that said what I wanted them to say, but He would always lead me to the scriptures about faith, strength, and hope.

"But without faith it is impossible to please Him, for he who comes to God must believe that He is, and that He is a rewarder of those who diligently seek Him" (Hebrews 11:6, NKJV).

"My flesh and my heart may fail; but God *is* the strength of my heart and my portion forever" (Psalm 73:26, NKJV).

"This I recall to my mind, therefore I have hope. *Through* the LORD's mercies we are not consumed, because His compassions fail not. *They* are new every morning; great *is* Your faithfulness. 'The LORD *is* my portion,' says my soul, 'therefore I hope in Him!' The LORD *is* good to those who wait for Him, to the soul *who* seeks Him" (Lamentations 3:21–25, NKJV).

As I was starting to slowly release the bars of control, I was finding it hard not to put all our trust in the doctors. I mean they had dealt with this Ugly Monster so many times. They knew what to expect, right? Or did they. Dustan was "unique," as the doctors put it. He never fell into the normal roadmap. Let's just say he did not follow the rules of the Ugly Monster ride, which made our ride into the unknown even more real.

The doctors gave us a roadmap of treatment to follow, but it seemed as if we were holding it up in the air and waiting to see if it would really get us to the end of our ride.

Our Journey Begins

We found out quickly the only true roadmap to follow was God's word. Don't misunderstand me. We still followed the doctors' instructions, but when things did not go just as planned, we knew our true roadmap was taking us to where we needed to go. We sought God daily for wisdom and guidance. We prayed for the doctors, nurses, and all the staff at VCH. If you are sitting in hospital rooms or clinic rooms for days on end, you have time. I could have chosen to think about all we were going through or think about my son lying there suffering. I chose to think on good things and to pray for all involved in my son's treatments.

"Finally, brethren, whatever things are true, whatever things *are* noble, whatever things *are* just, whatever things *are* pure, whatever things *are* lovely, whatever things *are* of good report, if *there is* any virtue and if *there is* anything praiseworthy—meditate on these things" (Philippians 4:8, NKJV).

Don't get me wrong; I did not always choose to see the bright side of the situation. There were days all I could see was what was in front of me, and I did not like it at all. It hurt to watch my son go through these painful procedures; it hurt to watch the medicines make him so sick he could not hold his head up. There were times he was so weak he could not even walk. Endless clinic visits and hospital stays continued, but I had to watch other children go through these same things. I had to look in the eyes of other parents knowing that they were feeling the same things I was. I had to not only watch, but also feel these same emotions. I hated it.

Some days it was so horrific I did not think I could do it. But you know what, I did not do it. Ultimately, it was Christ in me. I knew it was His Spirit manifesting in my life. There is no other answer but Christ in me. "I can do all things through Christ who strengthens me" (Philippians 4:13, NKJV).

I had realized that even though our family was in one cart on this Ugly Monster ride, there were so many other families in the carts ahead and behind us. Just as on a real roller-coaster, everyone is on the same track, but they do not react to the ride the same. Some did not even wear their safety harness. To me, this was God and His protection. My heart broke for these families on this ride with no protection. God would lay on my heart at different times to pray for certain families, and I would, eagerly.

Just as our family watched others go through what we were facing, we also knew that others were watching us. We knew if we were going to claim to have a relationship with Christ, then we needed to live it out before others. I can honestly say that Dustan did that so naturally. It was not an act to show others that he was strong; he really just lived it. Now to ask Dustan if he were strong, he would be the first to tell you he was not. The word "strong" in the Oxford Dictionary means "possessing skills and qualities that create a likelihood of success." That was my Dustan. He possessed tremendous skills and all the qualities that proved he would succeed.

The funny thing is, as Dustan was having to face all his fears, fear never showed to anyone else. All anyone else saw was his strength. Now that is what I call God working through us. Our fears are really what we consider our weaknesses. So is it not true that God shows mightiest in our weakest times?! God proved over and over again with Dustan and our family that if you give Him your fear and walk through that fear with Him, He will show you the value of your strength.

For instance, I told you that one of Dustan's biggest fears was needles. After being diagnosed, he had to have a Port-a-Cath placed in his chest. This was so that he would not have to have a needle placed in his arm every visit. However, to access his Port-a-Cath, he had to have a needle placed in this device each time. So a needle was pressed through his chest into the port. Not only did he have to face his fear and conquer it, he had to continually be reminded of this fear.

He did conquer it, although it never became comfortable to him. Just as in life. We may conquer one of our fears, but it does not mean that we are comfortable every time we are faced with it. We do know that we can face our fear, and we are better for it, but we are also reminded that with God living in us, we do not have to face it alone.

Facing life alone was unheard of in our family. Having two sons only twenty months apart, they were never alone. Dylan was energetic, fun-loving, a daredevil, and very strong-willed. His personality mixed perfectly with Dustan's laid-back, determined, giving, and compassionate heart. Dylan, being the youngest, looked up to his big brother and was never far from Dustan. As they got older, they stood together as a team. Rarely did they get in trouble separately. They always hung in there together and faced punishment and achievements as one.

While Dustan was having to face his fears, Dylan was having to adjust to his new role. Dylan had always been the fun-loving, take life as it comes kind of guy. He never took life too seriously. Why should he? Dustan was always the serious one. Dustan was very particular about everything in his life. He was organized, very detail-oriented, focused, quiet, and a great listener—but worried about everything. Dylan was the one that made everyone laugh and most everything came easily for him. I think because he never put that much pressure on himself, he just always did really well. He had his big brother to take care of him so he did not worry with all the minor details.

We used to laugh when they were younger because Dustan was so shy that Dylan would always make friends for both. Being so close in age, they were best friends; so others would just fit right into both their circles. They loved everything most young boys do: sports, running, jumping, and being loud. They were very competitive, but I really cannot think of any time that they physically fought. Dylan loved to wrestle and get tough but once anything got heated, Dustan would always walk away. I always said he was a lover not a fighter. Boy, would he prove me wrong. He was both!

There were many times we would all talk about who we thought could have handled having cancer better, Dustan or Dylan. Not that I wanted either to have to face this

RESTING IN HIM

battle. Watching your children grow up, you get this image of who you think they will be and what they can accomplish. As a mother, I thought I knew my children pretty well. I mean I had lived with them, nurtured them, and was training them to be good Christian young men. Who would know them better than I? Ahh, our heavenly Father! Of course, He knew them better than me. He had formed them in my womb. He knew them before I had even thought of their existence. Not only did He know them, He knew the men they were to become.

Truthfully, if you had asked our family, we would have said Dylan would be the one to handle cancer. Dustan, even though he was the big brother, was the one most timid and afraid of everything. He would crumble. He just could not do it. Little did we know of all the strength and bravery he would have for the battle of his life. So many times I would hear Dustan say: "I am glad it was me that got cancer and not Dylan." I'm not sure why exactly he felt that way. He never said. I just assumed he was the big brother and once again he was going to protect his brother at any cost. However, Dylan would prove later that *he* would protect his big brother at any cost.

Dylan was only thirteen years old when Dustan was diagnosed, and he had to take on some big responsibilities. Always having been the little brother, he now became almost like an only child. He had to grow up in ways he really did not want to. He had to go to school without his brother. Their entire lives they had been together. From preschool to high school, they had always been in the same place and surrounded with the same friends. Now, Dylan was not only facing school days without Dustan, he was also facing all the questions thrown at him:

"How is D-pan?* Is he feeling good today? When is he coming back?" And so on.

This was a constant reminder to Dylan that his big brother was no longer there for him to lean on. Their roles had somewhat reversed.

---

*Short for "Dustpan." All his schoolmates called him this. His name is pronounced "Dus-TAN," and when the ninth grade teacher first called roll, all the guys laughed and said, "Did you say 'Dustpan'?" From that time he was known as "Dustpan," and then it was shortened to D-pan.

Our Journey Begins

This might not seem so bad, but day after day, it gets to be a little much. Then he would come home, and Dustan was usually sick and did not feel like hanging out. Dylan after listening to all the questions all day really did not want to talk about it any more.

Then there were days we were not even home. We would be in the hospital, and Dylan would stay with friends. So they were starting to spend time apart, and we as a family were starting to have do things separately, which we had never done. We always did everything together. So this was new to all of us. None of us liked it, but we knew we were doing what we had to do to get through this Ugly Monster ride.

We all found out pretty quickly that the structure of our family was changing. We had to re-evaluate each other's role and pick up the slack when needed, to manage our new normal. We were all having to do things we did not want to do, and really not sure how to do it. Once you get on the ride, there is no getting off until the ride has come to a complete stop. So we had to figure out how to make the Ugly Monster ride a little more comfortable. As you know, when you are in that cart there are only so many ways to move around. So as we were adjusting ourselves in our assigned seats, the ride continued onward.

After many twists, turns, ups, and downs we had finally arrived on a straightway of the Ugly Monster. As Dustan and Dylan were moving ahead in their high school years, Kenny and I were trying to hold the family together the best we knew how. There were times we both felt like single parents. I was with Dustan mostly, and Kenny was with Dylan. Then on those rare, precious times we spent together as a family, we would try not to focus on the Ugly Monster but look out over the horizon to see what the future held for us.

Some days that was more difficult than others. There were days we could see everything so clearly; and then other days all we saw was the fog we were in. It was pretty easy for us to get caught up in the rituals of the Ugly Monster. I mean the newness of our normal was starting to wear off. It was becoming our life.

RESTING IN HIM

Life had become scary for me, as I thought all the things our family was experiencing were normal. How can this be normal? The things we were watching Dustan have to go through could not be considered normal! Recently, I looked up this word in the dictionary. It defined normal as, "conforming to a standard; usual, typical or expected." I could understand we were conforming to a standard, but typical or expected was not true of this Ugly Monster ride. At every turn we were facing the unexpected.

One time in particular about halfway through Dustan's treatments, we hit what I would call the ugliest part of the Ugly Monster ride. This was one of those not so typical or expected parts. No one saw this coming, not even the doctors. Out of nowhere Dustan started running a very high fever and was feeling more ill than normal. We had learned pretty early on, a temperature meant a trip to the emergency room; and most of the time that meant a hospital stay. So we always took a packed bag with us. Little did we know this would be a very long and painful hospital stay.

At first, it just seemed like Dustan had some type of infection, which was not unusual. He had faced those on many occasions. As the days passed Dustan was starting to be in extreme pain. His lips were starting to blister, other burnt places started showing up all over his body, and he was complaining that his stomach was hurting. We found ourselves just waiting. We were waiting for the doctors to determine what exactly was wrong with Dustan. Waiting and waiting....

Then the doctors discovered Dustan had a very bad reaction to one of his required chemotherapy medicines. So as the doctors were trying to find the best recourse, I was watching my son get worse. Not only was the outside of his body being burnt, he was being burnt from the inside out. I am talking about raw flesh. Literally, his hands, feet, and face were burnt and peeling. This medicine was trying to find a way to escape his body, so it was going from the top of his head all the way to the tip of his toes.

As I stated before, this was the ugliest part. Dustan's insides were starting to blister and flesh was starting to peel off his stomach, esophagus, throat, and mouth. This would make him deathly sick. He would have to throw up the excess skin. He could not eat or drink. Soon he could not even talk. Finally, they had to put him on a morphine pump. This was his only way to relieve the agony and to get any sleep.

Day after day I found myself sitting by Dustan's bed just sobbing; pleading with God to let me take this pain for my son. As I watched my son lying in this hospital bed with all these tubes and machines, I just could not believe that this was right or normal. Honestly, as I watched him deal with this Ugly Monster, I thought; "Oh, God, not even I could do this. How is Dustan enduring this extreme pain and this misery?" My heart would just break.

Let's just say, God and I were starting to have some real heart to heart conversations. He would always remind me that He was there and that He was my Comforter. But, I was feeling very alone and helpless.

During those days, Kenny would be at work, Dylan at school, and Dustan would sleep from the medicines. So it was just me and God during those difficult moments. I would try to leave the room just to get a little air, but I would not stay longer than a few minutes. I would think, "What if Dustan needs me and I am not there?" I may not be able to take the pain from him, but I was determined I would do whatever necessary to ease the pain.

It took weeks before Dustan started to get a little better. He was getting to where he could talk and function somewhat. The first words out of his mouth were, "I am sorry."

I said, "Sorry? What in the world do you have to be sorry for?"

He said, "I know I was grumpy and not fun to be around."

As the tears rolled down my cheeks, I grabbed his hand and looked into those deep blue eyes and said, "You were perfect."

RESTING IN HIM

Then he said, "Please do not let me forget to apologize to the nurses for being grumpy." I just looked at him with such amazement. How could this child have come from me? He had such compassion for others. The love of Jesus just flowed from him even as he was suffering.

My thoughts go to the crucifixion of Jesus. These men would take leather straps and strike Jesus over and over with them. His flesh would rip and bleed. What did Jesus say? "Father, forgive them, for they know not what they do" (Luke 23:34, NKJV). Dustan was not Jesus but he was doing as Jesus would, showing love and compassion for others as he was suffering.

> *Nails were not enough to hold God-and-Man nailed and fastened on the Cross, had not Love held Him there.*
> —CATHERINE OF SIENA

A father and son's love is unique—different from a mother's love. Kenny and Dustan were very close. They both shared the love of music and sports. Kenny had coached the boys in most of their sporting events. So when Dustan was taken to the emergency room when we first feared cancer, Kenny was with Dylan at a football game. As Kenny and Dylan were on the football field, Dustan and I were sitting there in the hospital room with questions being thrown at us like a dart game. I called Kenny immediately and told him all that was going on, and he said, "Just hang on, I will be there as soon as I can." It came to Kenny then, "How can I protect my son? I am here and he is there."

Once the realization of Dustan's diagnosis had settled in with Kenny, he was at his own personal crossroads. As a father you take on the responsibility of the protection of your family. So when your child becomes ill, your first thoughts are, How could I have let this happen? I saw Kenny struggle with what he thought he had done wrong or what he could have done different to prevent this. In reality, the answer was nothing. Just as with the rest of us, God was going to have take Kenny on his own personal journey of surrender. Surrendering not only his life, but his idea he knew what was best for his family. In other words, he was going to have to surrender his control (flesh).

Kenny was a pastor's kid, so he had grown up in the church. Not unlike most of your PKs, he had truly lived a very sheltered life. Throughout his life, he had several defining moments when God had spoken to him and had literally changed the direction of his life. Now he was in a crucial place where he had to find the right direction for himself and for our family. The life or death of our son depended on it.

I could see him struggling with the responsibilities of his everyday tasks. He had to work to provide for us and still held his responsibilities at church. He was torn on a daily basis as to what he had to put first: work, church, or his family. He had so much pressure placed on him, and he was trying to juggle so many things at once that I could see it was all getting ready to crash. I saw my husband and best friend of twenty years crumble under the pressure. He fell on his knees before God and surrendered his rights. He gave everything to God. It was a humbling experience for him. He came face to face with some major decisions that felt impossible.

But seek (aim at and strive after) first of all
His kingdom and His righteousness….
MATTHEW 6:33, AMPC

We had both been taught that if you put God first, then God will honor you and *these things* will be added to you. *These things* for us were wisdom and direction.

RESTING IN HIM

We were learning it was not about doing all the right things but seeking Him first, and doing everything God's way no matter the cost.

After much prayer and soul searching, Kenny had to make the decision that he was going to give God full control over his life and his family. He realized that it was not all about whether you are doing all the right things. It's about surrendering all of who you are to God and letting Him lead you in all His ways. Kenny knew that he would come up against some opposition, but he was assured (in complete peace) in his decision that he was in God's perfect will for him and us.

I will never forget that moment when Kenny stood in front of me, Dustan, and Dylan. His head was lowered, tears running down his face. He looked up at us three and said, "I am so sorry. I have failed each of you. I have been putting other things in front of you all. I have been trying to please everyone, and my family has paid the price. All I know is that I am miserable and I am tired of wrestling with God. I must do what is right and what God has asked of me."

He continued, "April, I am sorry you have had to watch Dustan go through all of this alone. I have not been the shoulder you needed to lean on. Dylan, I am sorry that you have had to spend so much time alone when you needed me as your father. Most importantly, Dustan, I am so very sorry I have not been by your bedside every time you needed me. I have put church and work responsibilities before you all. I have made a promise to God, and I am making a promise to you three. I will be the husband, father, and spiritual leader that God has called me to be."

God had dealt pretty directly with Kenny regarding his priorities. Now he put his relationship with God first, and then us, his family. It was not important to him any longer what others expected of him, but what God expected.

Kenny had finally found peace within the Ugly Monster. He was still learning to let go and let God, which I believe is a daily struggle of surrender of self for us all.

Our Journey Begins

"[I assure you] by the pride which I have in you in [your fellowship and union with] Christ Jesus our Lord, that I die daily [I face death every day and die to self]" (I Corinthians 15:31, AMPC).

I witnessed Kenny making a conscious choice to please God instead of man. Galatians 1:10 (AMPC) says, "Now am I trying to win the favor of men, or of God? Do I seek to please men? If I were still seeking popularity with men, I should not be a bond servant of Christ (the Messiah)."

All God was asking of Kenny was to walk a life pleasing to Him and to put Him first—to seek his guidance before seeking others'. I saw Kenny's relationship with his Father change. I saw his relationship with Dustan and Dylan blossom. I saw a man willing to be humbled and brought to his knees for his family's sake.

Even though we were just living life it was strange to me that this was really our life. I would walk through the days, weeks, and months sometimes not realizing how much time had passed. We were either at the clinic or in-patient in the hospital. So even though our life seemed to be going by quickly we found we were always in the state of waiting. Waiting for the medicines to work, waiting for the next procedure, waiting for the next test results, waiting to get out of the hospital. Then came the one that was the hardest, waiting for the end of the Ugly Monster ride.

All we wanted was this nightmare to end. It had only begun.

CHAPTER 3

Broken Dreams

*'My thoughts are not your thoughts,
and your ways are not my ways,' declares the Lord.*
(ISAIAH 55:8, GW)

It's been a long twenty-four months. Life was flowing pretty well—until we hit a brick wall. October 30, 2007, regular doctor visit—devastating news that afternoon. The doctor called to say, "RELAPSE." What, how, why? Was I surprised? Not sure. Devastated? Absolutely!

Lord, you know I believe. Why was it not enough this time? Has our journey been in vain? Have we not been through enough? Can we go again? I wasn't sure at first. God—where are you, I ask? I can't hear you—I can't see you—I can't feel you. OH, GOD! Do not forsake me now! It is you I need, it is you I crave. I search but can't seem to find any of the answers. Oh, God—I trust you!

RESTING IN HIM

David said in the Psalms, "My God, my God, why have you forsaken me? Why are you so far from saving me, so far from the words of my groaning?" (Psalm 22:1, NKJV).

What is worse than hearing your son has cancer? The word RELAPSE.

We had pretty much settled into the Ugly Monster and were finding the most comfortable way to endure this ride. Then our cart came to a wrenching halt. It was as if someone had put on the brakes but forgot to warn us. Thank goodness, we were wearing our safety harnesses (God's protection), because we would have surely been thrown from our seats.

Even still, we did not escape without injury. Our hearts were crushed, our arms fell to our sides, and all our hopes seemed to be shattered.

I remember that day I received the phone call that Dustan's cancer was back. When I heard the words CANCER and RELAPSE in the same sentence my heart stopped. I knew the Lord had prepared me that day. He had gently and sweetly revealed to me that Dustan was sick again. I just tried to fight that all too familiar queasy feeling. I kept pushing it away and saying, "God, I know this is not you telling me this." I should have known Who was speaking to me in that still small voice. I just did not want to believe it.

So I just went about my normal activities. Then the phone call came. The conversation seems as if it were yesterday. As soon as I said hello and heard the doctor's voice, I knew it was not good news. She quietly said, "April, are you sitting down?"

"Yes," I whispered.

She continued, "I am so sorry to say this, but Dustan's bloodwork is showing leukemia cells."

Broken Dreams

The only word I could say was "NO!" My heart was beating so fast in my chest I could not breathe. Inside I was yelling and screaming, "Oh, my God! No!" I knew she was talking to me, but I could not hear anything.

All I could get out of my mouth was, "Okay, what do we do now?" She talked for about ten minutes, of which I heard nothing. As we said goodbye I laid down the phone, fell to my knees, and cried tears of painful anguish. I remember asking God to give me the strength to share this terrible news with my family. I could hear Him say so gently, "April, you are not alone. I am here with you. You must trust me."

"Trust you!" I cried out. "Lord, I did trust you, and now my son is sick again." What does this word "trust" mean? That whatever happens is okay and I must accept it.

Exactly. Trust means "to commit to the safekeeping of" and "have a confidence; hope." I had committed Dustan to the Father for His safekeeping and I had the confidence and the hope that He would not fail us. I continually quoted Hebrews 10:23 (NASB), "Let us hold fast the confession of our hope without wavering, for He who promised is faithful." I knew my God was faithful. I was being assaulted with doubts as to whether His promises were true for us. I had to decide once again what was I going to trust: my feelings or my faith in God. I knew my feelings were not reliable, so I clung to my faith. I held fast to my confession of hope without wavering because He had promised and He was/is faithful.

The Lord had prepared not only me that day, but He had also prepared Dustan. When we went to our regular office visit that morning, Dustan shared with the doctors that he was not feeling right and they needed to do some tests. Just as Dustan knew in the very beginning that he had cancer, he knew his cancer was back. He was so brave that day when I told him of the doctor's phone call. He looked at me with those deep blue eyes and said, "Let's do it!"

RESTING IN HIM

After that, life became a whirlwind; our Ugly Monster had started to move forward again. This time it was much faster and with much more intensity. So our family of four grabbed hold of each other's hands, we placed our heels deep down, pushed ourselves back in our seats, and prepared for the next go-around on the Ugly Monster.

Soon after, Dustan and I found ourselves once again in the hospital. This time it would be a lengthy stay. Emotionally, I was having to wrap my mind around the new part of the Ugly Monster. I was having to prepare myself for the next ride. We had already set our sights on the end of the ride and were braced to take another trip around.

I knew God was there with us. I could still see His handprints all through our ordeal. I just could not understand, *Why again?* We were doing everything the doctors instructed. We were even doing it joyfully with smiles on our faces. *Now... you are asking Dustan to endure more?* Which included extreme chemotherapy, radiation, and a bone marrow transplant. *You are telling me our family is to take another trip around on the Ugly Monster? Not again.*

I found myself again on my face before God, seeking guidance and comfort.

"I called on Your name, O Lord, from the lowest pit. You have heard my voice: 'Do not hide Your ear from my sighing, from my cry for help.' You drew near on the day I called on You, and said, 'Do not fear!'" (Lamentations 3:55–57, NKJV)

As I was calling out from my pit, the Lord would continually give me, "Do not fear, I am with you always." He proved over and over again that He was riding along with us. Even though we would have to continue to ride this out, He would not leave us nor forsake us.

Every morning while Dustan slept I would visit the family quiet room. This room was full of windows and a great place to get away from the individual patient rooms. You could see the view of downtown. Most mornings I would read the

Broken Dreams

Bible, pray, and gaze out of the windows and dream, knowing that when I was done I would enter Dustan's room with a new perspective for the day. On many occasions I would write in my journal. These were my thoughts one morning:

Today as I look out of the window at all the people coming to work and going about their lives, I wonder what they are thinking or what is going on in their lives. They cannot see me in this room. They cannot see the pain of what I see. I sometimes want to hang out the window and yell, "YOU KNOW, LIFE COULD BE WORSE; BE HAPPY! YOU ARE BLESSED!!"

Oh well, people would not get it. Unless they have lived a tragedy they do not know the difference. I thank Jesus every day that I am where I am. Not thankful for Dustan being sick, just thankful for God's constant presence. Some days that is harder to feel than others. I am thankful that even through our circumstances I have grown spiritually. My biggest fear: falling back into that self-centered, stale Christian I was. I mean I loved the Lord with everything inside me. Then I figured out I did not have much inside me. Even though I talked about others and how they always said, "It's all about me," deep down that was me, too. I wanted what would make me happy. Sad; I did not even know what that was—things, I guess. Well, when your son's life is almost taken from you, THINGS do not matter. All that matters is survival. (You don't know what that is until you need it.)

I know I am rambling. Back to my biggest fear—being who I was before all this occurred (cancer). Even after we made it through the first phase of everything I thought I was different. Sitting on that same pew I had sat on so many times before was not the same. I had a restlessness in my soul—a hunger I cannot explain. Although I knew this and felt this way, yet I was sitting still on that pew. I claimed God was our healer and even shared this with people. But, I was quiet and still *about it.*

Then when I heard "relapse," I realized I can no longer be quiet and still. I must make a difference.

RESTING IN HIM

God draws mightily near to the praying soul.
To see God, to know God,
and to live for God—
these form the objective of all true praying.
—E.M. BOUNDS

I would love to tell you at that very moment my life changed drastically. It did not. I was starting a slow, painful process of surrendering all my dreams to the Father. Brokenness and surrender became my closest friends. They would change me if I was willing. I had a choice to make: was I going to sit quietly through this next ride of the Ugly Monster or was I going to willingly raise my hands towards heaven and be used by God?

I chose to be a willing vessel. I would describe myself as a cracked and broken pot. So as I started feeding myself with the word of God, what I was taking in was slipping out of the cracks to others: as only God can do. As Paul states in II Corinthians 4:7,8 (AMPC),

"However, we possess this precious treasure [the divine Light of the Gospel] in [frail, human] vessels of earth, that the grandeur and exceeding greatness of the power may be shown to be from God and not from ourselves. We are hedged in (pressed) on every side [troubled and oppressed in every way], but not cramped or crushed...."

Even though I may have felt pressed, crushed, and desperate I knew I was not alone. The Father was with me in every twist and turn of this Ugly Monster. My feelings would get the best of me on many occasions but I was learning to walk by faith and not by feelings. I knew that my feelings would lie to me, but my faith would stand firm, for it was based on God's word. God does not lie and His word will not return void (see Isaiah 55:11).

Broken Dreams

I would listen to praise and worship music, read encouraging and uplifting books, and talk with the Lord a lot. One day as I was listening to the words of a particular song it started me on my journey to finding God's love: my intimate relationship with the Father, the love I so desired and craved.

I wanted it to be a simple transaction: I ask God to heal, and within a reasonable timeframe, He gives me the miracle only He can give. But from God's perspective, we need to be shaped into something eternal; that's what happens only during the pressing, and the hedging in on every side. Yes, God desired my prayers; but it was not a transaction. It was for Him to give me more than what I was asking. The first thing, the one necessary thing, was for me to grow in intimacy with my true Father, the intimacy shown in the life of Christ.

There were a lot of days I would put a pretty smile on my face, but inside I was falling apart. All the painful things I had faced as a child, teenager, and young adult that I had so neatly tucked away were swirling around my mind. I was feeling worthless. I lived with accusations and heavy expectations; I believed the lies that I could never measure up.

I was empty, hungry, and broken. My son was lying in this hospital bed again. My husband and other son were off doing their daily activities. I was just trying to survive the pain I was walking in, and trying to make sense of all that was happening in our lives. I was learning that my dreams did not matter any more. All I wanted was what God had planned for us. My constant prayer was, "If my dreams do not line up with your desire then change my dreams, O Lord, change me."

I had often looked at Psalm 37:4 (NKJV), "Delight yourself also in the LORD, and He shall give you the desires of your heart," as the Lord giving me what I desired. One day as I was sitting in Dustan's hospital room the Lord revealed to me that His desire for Dustan and my desire for Dustan were one and the same: complete healing and restoration of his body. Although, my desire was not for Dustan to

RESTING IN HIM

have to endure the pain of this healing. The Lord was changing my desire to be His desire—for our family to be changed through this pain.

Broken dreams were becoming a part of our new normal. Hearing the word "relapse" was one of many times. The entire journey was one of broken dreams, from the day of Dustan's original diagnosis: the dream of my son being healthy and experiencing normal high school years; the future I had envisioned for Dustan and our family; the driving, dating, proms, sports—and, most importantly, watching him grow up to be a healthy man. Dreams crashing before my very eyes. How do you handle the devastation of your dreams? I was learning it painfully and daily: surrender.

God was taking me on my own personal journey of surrender. It was just me and my Father riding this part alone. I had been broken ("shattered, crushed") and now I was surrendering ("giving up claim to; give over or yield voluntarily, in favor of another") all my hopes and dreams.

Giving up something you have held onto for so many years can be impossible. God was asking me to pry my hands open and release what I thought I wanted, what I thought was best for Dustan and our family. Since I am a visual learner, God showed me my hands in a tight fist, and Him standing in front of me wanting to give me all that He desired for me and my family. If I could not release what I was holding onto then He could not place in my hands what He wanted to give: His love, His hope, His future. He would not force my hands open. I would have to willingly open them for Him.

In the book *A Divine Invitation*, by Steve McVey, he describes the connection between our sufferings and experiencing Christ: "It is often through suffering that God carries us deeper and deeper into an understanding of who we are in Him and Who He is in us." McVey also says, "Suffering causes the believer to become consumed with the desire to experience Jesus Christ! It makes us want to see Him, to hear His Voice, to feel His touch in our circumstances."

Broken Dreams

Wow! I think we would all choose to experience God through some avenue other than through suffering. But would we then devote our whole self to Christ? Something about Simon Peter's trial in the courtyard, plus his best friend's death, transformed his flawed faith into one that would flinch at nothing, not even at crucifixion.

As McVey notes, "Sometimes His most helpful acts in our lives occur when He goes through our circumstances with us instead of delivering us out of them."

It often takes the words of another to make you see the reality of your circumstance. As I was reading McVey's book I was discovering the love of Christ. I could not escape his love. Even in the fiery furnace of our circumstances his love quenched my thirsty soul. As I cried out in the midst of my pain, when He did not deliver me from my circumstances He would change my perspective on them.

Dustan already had the right perspective, as he wrote in his own words from his English paper:

High School Experience

As graduation approaches, seniors start to look back at their high school years. They start to remember exciting times they had with friends and teachers. They also remember all the sports games they went to, and all the funny moments of the past four years. People look at me and think I have missed "the high school experience," but it's just that my experience is different.

As a freshman, I was having a normal year of high school like everyone else. I was meeting new friends, because it was my first year at this school. I was getting to know my teachers and all the clubs. My freshman year was my only normal year of high school.

RESTING IN HIM

At first, my sophomore year was going exactly the way I wanted. I had all my classes, a lot of friends, and I was going to play basketball; but that was not the plan for my life. Right before basketball practice started, I was diagnosed with leukemia. This news basically ruined my sophomore year. The school did everything and anything it could to make me feel a part of my class that year, but it just didn't feel normal.

After going through a full year of chemotherapy, I was back at school for my junior year, and I was ready to make up for lost time. My junior year was somewhat normal, but I had a lot of issues that year. I would get an infection, or a classmate would come to school sick, or an appointment for the clinic would take all day. If I sat down and counted the days, I likely missed half my junior year.

Now this *year, my senior year was my year! I didn't have to worry about anything keeping me from enjoying it. As the year started, it was going great. I loved my classes, spent a lot of time with friends, and Coach C even asked me to be a student assistant coach; I was excited about that (I'm a better coach than player). But once again, that was not the plan for my life. I found that my leukemia had come back. I would be out for the rest of the year because of this. Again, the school did anything and everything to make me feel a part of the class, but, as I said before, it's not normal.*

Does that sound like a wonderful high school experience? Most people would say, "NO! That sounds like you were never at your high school." They are right; but what is a high school experience? It is being in the student section during a tense rivalry basketball game. Also, it's the relationship you had with your teachers and friends. What people don't understand is that I had that. I went to big games. I had relationships with friends and teachers.

But I've also had different high school experiences. I found out through all the hard times that I always had a school that loved me, and they would do anything and everything for me.

Broken Dreams

Now, when people come up to me and ask me, "Have you had 'the high school experience'?" I tell them, "Yeah, just not normal like you."

Dustan and I would discuss at length what I considered "broken dreams" and what he considered "God's plan." Even at the age of sixteen when he wrote this paper his perspective was far wiser than mine. He would say, "Mom, this is not what I wanted my teenage years to be, but I know that God knew all my days before I was born." I would smile with tears in my eyes and say, "I know." I was learning that God had divinely allowed every season of our lives in His sovereign wisdom, and each season has its own difficulties.

Dustan would prove to me on so many occasions that his perspective on "God's plan" was so clear, not only for himself, but for others. We would find ourselves in deep conversations on many nights while in the hospital. If you have never been in the hospital for long periods of time, then you do not know how lonely your nights can be. So being able to spend them talking with my son was priceless. I enjoyed his company probably more than he enjoyed my motherly protection. Many times he would let me know I could leave the room if I needed to.

Of course, I did not *need* to leave. True, he needed me; but I needed him more.

One night in particular I left the room for a few moments and went to my favorite place, the quiet room. While there I saw a mother I had seen so many times. Her son, whom I will call John, was ten.

She was on the phone speaking very quietly and sobbing uncontrollably. The only words I heard her speak were, "There is nothing else they can do. We have to just wait now, probably only days left."

As she got up to leave, she looked over at me, wiped the tears from her eyes, and even managed a slight smile.

RESTING IN HIM

I thought, how can you smile? My heart ached for this family, especially this mother.

I sat there frozen, and not a word did I speak to this mother. I could not move. I wanted to run as fast as I could to my room. I was thinking, What do you say to a mother who knows her child only has days to live? Fear gripped my heart. All I could do was pray for this family, praying God would give them peace and comfort for their anguished souls.

As I slowly got up to go back to the room, I could feel the tears flowing from my face. I tried to fight them off as much as I could. When I entered Dustan's room he knew something was wrong. I had to explain to him that another one of his sojourners was not going to be cured—that John only had days left to live.

As I was trying to get myself back under control Dustan and I started talking about this boy. John had received the news that day his tumor was growing rapidly and there was nothing else the doctors could do. As I was explaining to Dustan what I had just seen moments before, he looked up at me and said, "Mom, I am sure the Lord prepared John."

My heart leaped out of my chest. How do you prepare a child to go to heaven? How do you prepare, as parents, to let go of your child? I looked at Dustan with tears in my eyes and said, "God's love is amazing and I am sure He prepares His children for their entrance into heaven." I just cannot imagine, and I did not want to entertain that thought.

I sought the Lord that night for some peace for my troubled soul. I was reminded of a reading earlier that week from my *Hinds' Feet on High Places* devotional. It was called "Holy Detour."

"When there appears to be a contradiction between what God has promised and what we see happening, remember that we see from a limited perspective.

Broken Dreams

We see, as it were, only one narrow slice out of the whole pie of life. God, though, sees it all—His knowledge is perfect."

She goes on to say, "Losing one's life is painful. It's death! Upon hearing a missionary's report of God's work, a woman commented, 'I'd give my life to be used like that!' The missionary replied, 'That's what it would cost!'"

Those words hit me like a ton of bricks. We are expected to die daily—die to self. I was having to remind myself to have God's perspective, not mine.

A few days later the news of John had swept the entire floor. Everyone knew. Emotions were very high. The floor was filling up with all the nurses loving on John, other parents trying not to think that could be their child, and John's many relatives coming to visit. I preferred not to leave the room. I started losing myself in my own emotions. Dustan did not say much, but I knew he was thinking of John.

These were my painful words as I wrote them the night John went to be with his heavenly Father:

The Lord gave me Psalm 77 today. How powerful these words are to me even though written so many years ago. My heart has been overwhelmed with heaviness. All I can think about is John and his family. The agony they must be going through. John is so brave—he has such a peace about going to heaven. As a mother, how do you deal with this pain? You want to enjoy each passing moment and yet you want to stop living. I am sure she wants to stop TIME and give John more time.

I have let my mind go there way too often. This whole week I have struggled with emotions I do not even want to admit. Dustan is doing so good. I am thrilled God is answering our prayers. God keeps reminding me that He has a plan for Dustan. It does not include going to heaven just yet. He wants to accomplish many things through him. God does remind me of this often.

RESTING IN HIM

I keep losing my thoughts back to John and his family. I read his Carepage update and my heart sank. Yesterday when I read he wanted to be baptized and his pastor came to the hospital and baptized him in the bathtub—that is all my heart could take. I went and got alone and lost complete control. Again, my precious Father reminded me that this is not Dustan. Then I wept harder.

The whole day yesterday was difficult. Even when I went to bed my eyes would not close, my heart would not stop hurting. So this morning when the Lord gave me this scripture, AGAIN I lost control. Oh, how only you know my heart. Oh, how you know my agony. Thank you, Lord, that you love me enough to take me in your precious arms and remind me continuously you are in control.

Psalm 77: 1–4 (NKJV). I write this and weep:

I cried out to God with my voice—
To God with my voice;
And He gave ear to me.
In the day of my trouble I sought the Lord;
My hand was stretched out in the night without ceasing;
My soul refused to be comforted.
I remembered God, and was troubled;
I complained, and my spirit was overwhelmed.
Selah
You hold my eyelids open;
I am so troubled that I cannot speak.

The night before as I lay on my makeshift bed, the hospital couch, my eyes would not close, my heart could not be comforted, and my spirit was screaming to God. Only my Father who loved me more than anyone else would know my grieving soul. He saw my heart when no one else could. He knew I might not admit to others but my heart was screaming out, "Have compassion and mercy on my troubled soul."

Broken Dreams

*Through the Lord's mercies
we are not consumed,
because His compassions fail not.*
(LAMENTATIONS 3:22, NKJV)

We had found ourselves upside down in this Ugly Monster again, and I was trying hard to catch my breath. We were in one of those delayed moments when you could actually look around and see all that was going on around you. The scene was horrific. Too many children were losing their battle with the Ugly Monster and I had to watch. No longer strangers, all these people had become like family. I was watching the Ugly Monster wreak havoc. Even though my heart was troubled by what it cost my son to fight, I still wanted him to fight as hard as he could. Watching all these determined children face off the Ugly Monster, only to lose, was more than my heart could stand.

I kept asking God, "Why must I watch these precious children and their families suffer? What can I do to help?"

He would answer, "Love them."

The funny thing is before our journey began I was a very private person. Never did I share my thoughts or feelings with anyone. Isn't it just like God to make us stretch out of our comfort zone? He was asking me to love people. I was struggling just to survive from day to day, and now I had to use my energy to love others.

I had learned a lot up to this point. One fundamental lesson was that I must learn to be honest and transparent with my fellow Christians. If not, can I give glory to God? If I excluded others, then they would never see God's beautiful work along our path.

RESTING IN HIM

You see, God had taught me that we are all the same. We all want others to see us as we wish ourselves to be. God knows who we really are and HE still loves us. Lesson learned, if we are open and honest with ourselves then God can use us mightily.

Let me take you on a little journey with me. I want you to imagine you are in a dark room trying to find the light. You bump into unfamiliar things and you feel your heart racing. Fear grips you.

Suddenly you feel this breath against the back of your neck. Your eyes will not adjust to the darkness; you're not sure Who is with you. You try to slip away from this unknown Being, but your feet will not move fast enough! Whichever way you go, still you feel this breath on your neck.

Panicking, you reach out to feel Who is there—to no avail; you feel no one. You frantically hunt the light switch. This breath feels stronger. You trip and fall; you realize you are stuck and cannot get up. You have a decision to make, do you stay down or do you call out to this mysterious Being?

This breath feels nearer. What do you do? For some odd reason your eyes still will not adjust. In terror you decide to call out, "Who is there?" You hear nothing. You say it again, "WHO is there?"

Unexpectedly, arms lift you up and help you to your feet. You still cannot see anyone, but you recognize that breath. It is the One you felt while in the dark. Saying nothing, It leads you toward a small light on the other side of the room. You still feel Its breath and very strong arms as It leads you toward the light. Once across to the small light, you realize the breath and the strong arms are gone. You do not know exactly when they left you. You just know that they saved you from the darkness. You look back over your shoulder in the pitch-black room and know you would have never made it without their help.

Broken Dreams

This was my experience with the Holy Spirit. I had been walking in darkness searching for the true light (the truth of God's word). I had been stumbling on what I thought the truth was and bumping into religion. As I walked through these dark places in my life, I knew something was there; I just could not find it. I could not put my hands on it.

Then, watching all these other children losing their battle with the Ugly Monster, at one point I could not see any truth. So I cried out to the breath I had felt so many times in my darkness. And It came and rescued me. It took me to the light (truth) of God's unfailing love. Sometimes we may find the light ourselves and turn it on, but it's when the Holy Spirit guides us to the light that we really see the truth.

It's the truth of the cross. He loved us so unconditionally, He gave His only Son so that we may have life, and have it more abundantly. His one true desire from us is worship. He wants us to love.

I had learned no matter what dreams I previously had, nothing matters more to me than my love relationship with my heavenly Father. He showed me my dreams might have been broken, but His dreams for Dustan and our family were bigger than mine.

Ephesians 3:20 (AMPC) says it best, "Now to Him Who, by (in consequence of) the [action of His] power that is at work within us, is able to [carry out His purpose and] do superabundantly, far over *and* above all that we [dare] ask or think [infinitely beyond our highest prayers, desires, thoughts, hopes, or dreams]...."

He revealed to me that He has so much in store for my family, more than I could have ever dreamed possible.

CHAPTER 4

Rope of Hope

*There I will give her back her vineyards,
and will make the Valley of Achor a door of hope.
There she will respond as in the days of her youth,
as in the day she came up out of Egypt.*
(HOSEA 2:15, NIV)

Now let me give glory where glory is due. My precious heavenly Father! There have been days that I wondered where my God was and then there were days I knew exactly where He was—wherever I was. I have not walked this journey perfectly, but I have walked and sometimes crawled this journey the only way I knew how—with my precious heavenly Father by my side. If it were not for Him I could never have made it this far. There are days I cannot wait for the night to come so that I can go to sleep and hope for a better tomorrow. Then there are days I never want to see the night come because the day is so perfect. All I know is each day with Him is the day He planned for me.

RESTING IN HIM

So again let me give glory where glory is due: Praise You, Lord, and only You! For any of you who read my words, if you do not have a personal relationship with our heavenly Father or you have fallen away, please do not let time slip by. If I have learned anything from our journey it is that my Father loves me and my family unconditionally. He gave His only Son that I may have life. For me to watch my son almost lose his life and know that I wasn't giving him up without a fight—how much more could our Father love us, that He gave up His Son so freely? Oh, that I can only be a witness to His awesome power! His healing power! I shall be forever changed. (John 3:16.)

Resting in Him, April

God's love and the love of His people had become our Rope of Hope. It was still our family of four riding this Ugly Monster, but every time we would get near the bottom, there it would be, our Rope.

We would grab it and wrap it around ourselves securely, so as to make the next go around. Until then, a rope was a length of strong cord twisted together of natural fibers. Now, as I saw the supernatural fiber of many hearts all united into one strong love, there was a new kind of "rope." Our Rope had become part of our survival in the journey of the Ugly Monster.

In Chapter 1, I had mentioned God had placed us at Mt. Juliet Christian Academy, and how the students, parents, and faculty would play an intricate role in our journey. I want to show you how a normal fifteen-year-old boy, who happened to be my son, brought a school and community together in love. First, let me share how God orchestrated our lives to include MJCA.

One day as I was driving through Mt. Juliet, Tennessee, I passed by the First Baptist Church, which also housed Mt. Juliet Christian Academy. So clearly I heard this thought in my head that I knew was from God, "Your boys will be attending that school."

Rope of Hope

I laughed at that thought. You see, my boys were at another Christian School, and had been since preschool. We were all very happy there and had no plans on leaving our current school. So I quickly dismissed the thought. Funny how the Lord can be very persistent. Every time I passed by the school the Lord would remind me, That is where your boys will be attending. For nearly six months I felt an urging to look at this school. Finally one day I said, "Okay, Lord, if you insist. I will check this school out, but you will have to convince the rest of the family." Knowing everyone else in the family would say, No way!

After doing much research, a lot of prayer, and God really changing the desire of my heart, I decided to approach Kenny with this idea. I knew it would not go over very well unless the Lord had already been doing some behind the scenes work. I wasn't surprised when I mentioned it to Kenny and he said, "No, why would you want to change schools?" I then proceeded to tell him of my conversation with God and how this urging would not go away. He said, "Okay, let's just pray about for a while." Then within the week Kenny came back to me and said, "I feel like we need to visit the school." We decided not to say anything to the boys just in case we were wrong. God knew He was not wrong; He had already planned our footsteps even if we thought it was our decision. So we made our visitation appointment, not really knowing that day would change the course of our lives.

Walking in the school that day Kenny and I both felt the love of the Lord very strongly. We were taken on a tour and then met with one of the administrators. After much discussion of the school's mission statement and vision, we all prayed together, and then Kenny and I left to make our decision. As Kenny and I walked out the door that day we looked at each other knowing without a doubt that our boys would be attending this school.

Now, the hard part would be explaining to our boys that they would be changing schools. Spring break was fast approaching, so we decided to let Dustan and Dylan tour the school then.

RESTING IN HIM

I will not go into a lot of details of our preparation for the change of schools but I will tell you Dylan was very excited and Dustan was devastated. Remember, Dustan was afraid of the unknown. So he was terrified by the thought of making new friends, meeting new teachers, and just the size of this much bigger school. Dylan, on the other hand, was thinking — something new and exciting! So there were many mixed emotions at our house that summer: Dylan talking all the time of the adventures of his new school, and Dustan saying, "Dylan, you can go, BUT I WILL NOT GO! Mom and Dad cannot make me!"

Knowing Dustan's love of music, I wanted to get him involved in the marching band to make the transition easier. Band practices started several weeks before school. As a mother, I was trying to be helpful and get him established before the first day of school arrived. But, on the day of the first band practice, to my horror, Dustan refused to get in the car.

Dustan had never rebelled against my authority. So I was shocked when he looked at me with those sweet baby blues and said, "I will not get in that car and you cannot make me."

I looked at him and said, "If I have to pick you up and place you in that car, I will. Now get in that car!" Now Dustan was fourteen years old, about 5' 3", and 140 pounds. I knew I could not pick him up. But I was surely going to try if I had to. So the battle was on.

Let's just say I won, but took no pleasure in winning. It broke my heart to see him so afraid of something I knew would be great for him, a move I knew God was orchestrating.

I am reminded of the story of Jonah and the great fish. Jonah did not want to obey the voice of the Lord. He did not want to go where the Lord needed him to go. Jonah could not trust God with the outcome of His request to go to Nineveh,

Rope of Hope

so he fled. Just like most of us. We fear what the result will be if we follow God's plan. We with our earthly eyes have already envisioned the outcome—when in reality we have no way of knowing what God has planned for us. If we trust in God's love for us, should we not rest assured that whatever He asks of us is for our divine purpose? God used Jonah in spite of himself and He would also use Dustan.

It took several months for Dustan to become comfortable with his new surroundings. Everyone at MJCA just embraced him, and he quickly became a part of this new family. To my surprise, one day out of the blue he came up to me, put his arms around me, and said with his sweet soft voice, "Mom, thank you."

I said, "For what?"

He said, "For making me go to my new school. I know I was mean to you, but you loved me enough to make me do it. I so love you for that."

Tears filled my eyes as he ran off. I then realized sometimes we have to do things that are painful for our children, but it is for their growth. That day prepared me for all the other days I would have to encourage him to do things he really was not comfortable with doing. I describe these events so you can see how Dustan was going to have to grow and trust God for the direction in his own life. Then, through his growth, so many other lives would be touched. It was just a small piece of God's bigger plan, but it would prove to be significant.

From the first moment that MJCA heard of Dustan's diagnosis, it started a whirlwind of activities. From the high school boys shaving their heads (since Dustan would be losing his hair), to weekly food drop-offs, tutoring, many home and hospital visits, cards, money, fundraisers—and the list goes on and on. These families became our family. We were so overwhelmed with the show of God's love and kindness.

RESTING IN HIM

Throughout our entire journey we were bathed with prayer. We knew God had placed us there for such a time as this. We just did not realize how much Dustan would impact their lives in return.

Dustan had become a part of everyone's lives, not just his fellow friends in high school but the entire school body. For someone who missed a lot of school days he was never far from anyone's thoughts. Not a day passed that someone did not call or text him with well wishes. Then when he was at school he was surrounded with encouragement and love from everyone. There were so many days he would go to school when he was physically exhausted and in so much pain that my heart would ache for him. He would pull himself out of the bed and get dressed while throwing up. I would say, "Are you sure you can do it?"

He would put that big smile on his face and say, "You bet." Dustan and Dylan would hop in the car and off they would go. I would watch as they drove off and then I would hit my knees. Praying God would watch over them both.

I never wondered where God was, because I knew that we talked most every minute of every day. Every moment that Dustan was out of my sight I knew God was holding him. I mean, how else could he have put one foot in front of the other if it were not for God? It was almost humanly impossible to walk the path he did.

I remember one morning when he was having a test in his AP history class. He had been sick most of the night, so when I went into his room that morning I just knew he would not be able to get up. To my surprise, he was already dressed and putting his shoes on. I tried to convince him to stay home, but he ignored my requests. He said, "I cannot get behind in my school work. I will be fine."

I cannot tell you how many school mornings I watched amazed at his strength and determination. Not only did I see it, but his entire school saw it when he walked through those doors with a huge smile on his face. Then with a quick hello and an encouraging word for everyone he saw, he would be off about his day. No one knew what he had faced the night before or that morning just trying to get to school. He never shared his struggles with anyone. He would just smile through it and place his trust in God. He would often say, "You know, my friends have their own problems; they do not need to hear about mine."

Dustan did not like to be the center of attention. He liked to fade into the background. MJCA would not let this happen. They always showed their support and heartfelt love of him. Just like the time we were in the hospital and Dustan received a phone call from his brother, Dylan, telling him to go to the family quiet room and look out the window. Because of Dustan's immune system he was not allowed visitors; we were amazed to see a huge group of his fellow students, teachers, and parents on top of the parking garage roof across the street. As we looked out the window everyone started cheering Dustan's name and holding up signs which read, "We love Dustan!" and "We miss you!" Then, one by one, each person passed around the cell phone and spoke to Dustan individually.

Dustan being the quiet, humble person that he was could not believe these people would take time out of their day to come visit him. All the nurses were loving on Dustan and telling him how special he must be for everyone to come see him. He would just smile and with a quick, nervous laugh say, "I can't believe it's just for me." The people in that cheering crowd may have thought they were making a very small gesture. For Dustan and our family it was another strong wrap from our Rope of Hope.

They brought us a living depiction of the one mind and one voice Romans 15:5,6 (NASB) describes: "Now may the God who gives perseverance and encouragement grant you to be of the same mind with one another according to Christ Jesus, so that with one accord you may with one voice glorify the God and Father of our Lord Jesus Christ."

RESTING IN HIM

Nothing encourages our brothers and sisters in Christ more than enduring with them their hardships. MJCA was showing us how it's done.

Every rope has two ends. We were wrapping ourselves with our end, and MJCA was wrapping themselves with their end. Our relationships were beginning to bond and Dustan was the common knot between us all. Dustan's love and faith in the Lord would become the window people would view our journey through. He would stand strong and steadfast in his faith. He would declare his love for the Lord like none other. He proclaimed that no matter what his circumstances, he was an overcomer through Christ. On so many occasions through his pain, he would make it through and he would endure with joy. MJCA would see this giant of faith—and I would see a teenager trying to find his own faith in dealing with the Ugly Monster.

As babies learn to walk, building faith in children works the same way. They start out by holding the hands and walking on the feet of their parents (the parents' faith). As children grow, they must next learn to walk out their own journey of faith. There is a time they must let go of their parents' hands and step off their parents' feet. It is where they find their own footing in their walk of faith. They will stumble and fall, but as they learn to look to their Father and their focus becomes secure they will learn to walk uprightly with confidence. I was watching my son slip from my hands of faith into my Father's hands of faith. It was a humbling experience.

And He set my feet upon a rock
making my footsteps firm.
(PSALM 40:2, NASB)

As we are walking our daily walk we do not realize the people we are ministering to. Every day you have to make a decision how you are going to handle the triumphs and hardships of that day. The decisions you make, the paths you choose,

Rope of Hope

will ultimately give rise to someone else's lesson. So many days when our family was experiencing the upside-down turns of the Ugly Monster we were unaware of all those bystanders watching our ride. We were just trying to hang on and survive without falling. It was our constant Rope of Hope—God's truth and our brothers and sisters in Christ—that would keep us grounded in our seats. The Father was so faithful in providing for our every need: financially, emotionally, and spiritually.

God amazes me how He will provide these needs. One day in particular after I had experienced a very hard emotional hit, I was waiting for an elevator on Dustan's floor at the hospital. Two men walked up and talked among themselves until the elevator arrived. When stepping on the elevator the younger of the two asked me, "Have you been here a while?"

I replied, "Yes, and it will probably be a while longer." The older gentleman started telling me his story. He had been diagnosed with tumors on his brain years before. The doctors told him he must have the tumors removed, but where they were located required complex surgery. He decided that he would do chemotherapy and not have the surgery. Many treatments later, the tumors were not going away. The doctors gave him little hope. So he said he and his family just prayed. When he returned for a follow-up test, the tumors were still there. They had gotten smaller, though. Even up to this day, he said, the tumors were there; but he was fine. He believed that was God's reminder to him that the circumstances may not change but he could walk through them. To the doctors' amazement, even though the tumors remained he was still a very healthy man. He believed he was healed.

After he gave me his testimony, the younger man (I believe he was his son) looked at me and said, "Your son will be fine. It may not look like it now but he will leave this hospital and his life will be a testimony to many."

I stopped dead in my tracks and looked at him with amazement. I said, "How did you know I had a son that was sick? I did not tell you that."

RESTING IN HIM

He looked at me and said, "God told me," then smiled.

I was meeting Kenny downstairs, so I ran over where he was. It was just a few steps away. I excitedly said, "Come meet these two men and let them tell you their story."

But we turned around, and the two men were gone—nowhere to be found. The funny thing was, there was really no route for them to leave the building without going past us. They had not passed by us. Were they angels? Maybe, or maybe not—that day they were my angels. I needed the encouragement that my son was going to be okay. I needed to know, after watching so many other children lose their battles, there was still hope for my son.

Romans 15:13 (ESV), "May the God of hope fill you with all joy and peace in believing, so that by the power of the Holy Spirit you may abound in hope." My hope had been renewed that day, just from this one man's testimony. Never underestimate the power of your words or your testimony.

Looking at your circumstances won't always give you reason to hope. You must look beyond them to see from God's perspective. Trials in our lives help increase our faith. Just like our physical muscles, our spiritual muscles must be exercised to build our faith. Hope will never disappoint (Romans 5:5). Our Rope was helping to build our faith; and we were not going to be disappointed.

God uses so many ways to build hope. I had experienced hope through family, friends, and strangers; but my most cherished way was through God's love. I had often heard people say you do not have to be alone to be lonely. You can be in a crowd of people and feel you are the only one there. This was my experience with the Ugly Monster. I could be surrounded by so many people, but held captive by my thoughts. People talking of their everyday lives and what was going on—I could not grasp the fact of their everydayness. I was drowning in my own thoughts. It was as if I were in the ocean and floating with the waves, some days peacefully;

Rope of Hope

then, other days, I would fall off my life preserver, God's word. Then I would just bob up and down gasping for breath, struggling to hold onto to the truth of God's word. Eventually, I would feel this Rope and I would start to wrap it around myself. Once I was completely wrapped with the Rope I could pull myself back up onto my life preserver and began to catch my breath again.

Learning to breathe was a new concept for me. I had done it so naturally through the years. Now I caught myself listening to my own breath to see if I were truly living or not. Then I would catch myself watching to see if Dustan was breathing.

Sometimes he saw me watching him. He would smile and say, "I am fine, Mom."

I would always say, "I know you are, but I love to watch you anyways." He would sweetly laugh at me, but I knew he was tired of being on display. I watched his every moment, his every breath, and his every movement. Not sure what I was looking for; just wanted to be prepared if he needed me. I had not realized it just yet, but Dustan was also part of my Rope of Hope. Dustan and I had spent most of our waking and sleeping hours together; as I was learning to deal with my thoughts, I am sure Dustan was, also. Dustan was not a chatterbox, so when he spoke it was usually something significant. I was finding out that Dustan was much wiser than his years.

Often put, he was an old soul in a young body.

My conversations in the hospital with Dustan had become some of my treasured times. We would talk about his school, his classmates, and how his high school years were turning out. He would share with me about how his friends would ask him how he really was handling all that was happening to him. How they thought he was so strong and brave. He would look at me very intently and say, "You know, I am not that strong."

RESTING IN HIM

Of course, I would deny it. I would grab his hand and say, "You are the strongest person I know. You may not see it but we all see it."

He would say, "Not me, Mom."

I would reassure him that he was, and that he was "my hero."

He would say, "That is what everyone at school calls me, and they say I am such an inspiration to them. It must be Christ, because I do not see it."

I saw it, and Dustan was right; it was Christ. He and I could not see Christ in ourselves, but others could. There were times people would come to visit and I would smile and nod as if I really understood what they were saying. I heard comments like, "You are so strong, I just don't know how you do it. If it were me I would crumble."

I know most people do not know what to say and they really saw this as the truth. I saw it as if I were living a lie. Like Dustan, I saw myself as none of these things. All I could see was the hell we were living in. I was trying to figure out how my thoughts could line up with the truth of what others were seeing in me. I was not strong, I was not doing anything special, and I wanted to crumble.

The truth is, what others were seeing in me was Christ. I was dying on the inside, but God's love was being manifest to others on the outside. I do not say this to be boastful, but only to the glory of God.

Ephesians 2:9 (AMPC), "Not because of works [not the fulfillment of the Law's demands], lest any man should boast. [It is not the result of what anyone can possibly do, so no one can pride himself in it or take glory to himself.]"

This verse states what we do is not of ourselves, or so-called works, but it is Christ in us. This was part of what God was revealing to me as my own personal nugget.

Rope of Hope

It is not of myself. It is not what I can do. It is what He can do through me. I had heard this so many times in my Christian walk; I really even thought I was living this out daily. Not until I was forced to truly live it did I know the impact of Christ in me.

I was having to learn this, and so was Dustan. On those many days our thoughts would try to hold us captive, our Father would be faithful in giving us hope—hope in Him, His truth, and His promises. We would have to fight a spiritual battle daily. Truth against lies. The Father (truth) versus satan (father of lies). We knew the end of the story. We knew the Father wins. We just had to constantly renew our mind with the truth.

> *And be constantly renewed in the spirit of your mind [having a fresh mental and spiritual attitude].*
> (EPHESIANS 4:23, AMPC)

Now if anyone knew the meaning of a fresh mental and spiritual attitude, it would be Dustan. He had so many occasions to be downhearted and to wallow in some self-pity. Honestly, I think I would have visited my own pity party. Not Dustan; he chose to see the light at the end of the tunnel every single time.

On one of those occasions when I would have given up, he chose the higher road and won the battle. Let me explain.

Midway through his treatments he was diagnosed with *avascular necrosis*, or bone infarcation; this is where there can be tiny breaks called "microfractures." The fractures can cause the bones to collapse. Although your bones can grow back together in time, you still have to be extremely careful not to break any bones. For Dustan this occurred in his feet. This meant he had to wear protective boots and be

RESTING IN HIM

in a wheelchair.

This is devastating to a teenager on many levels. For Dustan, this meant he would have to go to school in a wheelchair, and he would not be able to play drums in the praise and worship band at church.

Dustan decided pretty quickly that this would not be his truth. He would not wear the boots, and he was going to play the drums at church. Being the protective mother that I am, I said, "Uh, I do not think so." I was concerned that if he broke any of his bones they would not heal back correctly and this would cause permanent damage to his feet.

If I thought I was determined that he was not going to play, Dustan was more determined that he *was*. So after a long, loving conversation, we made a deal. He would go to school and stay in the wheelchair (which he hated) if I would let him play the drums. I agreed.

It was something Dustan said to me that sealed the deal. He said with such wisdom, at a depth I have never seen before in him, "Mom, you know the drums are my passion. It is what gets me through the hard parts of this journey. If God loves me as much as I know that He does, and He knows my heart's desire is to play for Him, He will protect my feet."

How can you say no to that? His trust in the Lord was so evident that I could not deny him his heart's desire, to play to an audience of one, his heavenly Father.

As far as the deal, Dustan benefited from both. He got to play the drums, and did so with a newfound passion. Also, he found the silver lining to having to use a wheelchair at school. His friends would accompany him to all his classes. If his class just happened to be upstairs they would carry him on their backs up the stairs. This was true friendship—even though they did get out of class early. Dustan would come home and tell me of the day's events with such a sparkle in his eye. He would say, "I had such a great day. Hope my friends did not mind taking care of me." Dustan's friends never saw him as a burden; all they saw was a leader. The entire school rallied around him during this time and made him feel comfortable even though he had found himself with a few more obstacles with the Ugly Monster. Dustan and the Ugly Monster would battle many more times after this, but Dustan would always prove that his faith was the light in the darkness.

Darkness is a scary thing, and it can take many forms. It can be the partial or full absence of light, unhappiness or distress, lack of spiritual or intellectual enlightenment. In whatever form, darkness can be overcome. Bringing light into the darkness will eventually reveal all that has been hidden.

There were times we had to squint to see the light. We knew the light was there; it was just too difficult at times to see the truth of all that was happening. As our faith strengthened, our light shone brighter—not only for us to see His truth, but for others to see Christ in us. It was not until the truth was revealed to me by the Father that I could walk in His freedom—freedom from the bondage and darkness of the lies. I have come to cherish three themes found in Ephesians 5: 1–17 (NKJV): Walk in love; walk in light; walk in wisdom.

Verse 14 celebrates the glory of our relationship with Jesus. The light that shines comes from Him, as we walk with Him:
> "Awake, you who sleep,
> Arise from the dead,
> And Christ will give you light."

I was starting to know my Father in the way He had planned from the beginning of time. It was all about a true, intimate relationship. It was not about religion any more. It was about the love shared between my Father and me.

It was what I had been missing all along, the intimacy. I had been striving to live my Christian life through my own strength. He was showing me that it was through His life in me that I can come to truly understand the abundant life He speaks of in scripture. It all began with love, the love of the Father—and now, me sharing this love with my son.

My Rope of Hope was beginning to strengthen. So with each dip, twist, and jerk of disappointments we endured I found it easier to climb up out of the pits of darkness, loneliness, and despair. It was always my choice whether to stay wrapped with my Rope of love and truth, or to just let go. I would choose to hold on. For I knew the love of my Father would not fail me.

Billy Graham once said, "The promises of God's love and forgiveness are as real, as sure, as positive as human words can make them. But just as the total beauty of the ocean cannot be understood until it is seen, God's love cannot be understood until you experience it, until you actually possess it. No one can fully describe the wonders of God's love."

We should never question God's great love; it is just who He is. If it were not for the love of God, we would never experience our future in eternity. God is love and His love for each of us is everlasting.

Jeremiah 31:3 (NIV) is one of my favorite scriptures: "The Lord appeared to us in the past, saying: 'I have loved you with an everlasting love; I have drawn you with lovingkindness.'"

We can let a rope entangle us or help set us free. It is always our choice. God provides our ropes: His word, His people, others' testimonies, but most importantly Himself. Our hope is found in Him. "God wanted to make known to those among the Gentiles the glorious wealth of this mystery, which is Christ in you, the hope of glory" (Colossians 1:27, HCSB). Don't get tripped up by the ropes of despair, discouragement, and distraction. Those ropes can keep you entangled in hopelessness and confusion. By keeping your eyes on Jesus and wrapping yourself with His love you can be set free to trust His ways and His timing.

A song by Mercy Me, "Never Alone," is the conversation I was having with the Father as I made it through the days and nights: *"Hope, don't be a stranger,"* the narrator cries out.

> *Then a voice comes calling out to me,*
> *'You're never alone, 'cause I am with you.*
> *And I will always be.'*

I could not make it if my eyes remained on myself, or on what each day might bring. Our hope is in Him. He will never leave us and His love will always be a part of us. When we keep our eyes on Him even when doubting, our hope can be fulfilled because of His love and faithfulness.

CHAPTER 5

Brotherly Love

*Be tender loving one to another with brotherly love;
in honor preferring one another.*
(ROMANS 12:10, KJ2000)

Dear Friends,
Here we go again. We are back in the hospital. Today is Day 2 of chemo. Dustan is doing fairly well. He is sleeping mostly. "Better to sleep than to be sick" is his motto. So I just let him sleep the chemo away.

This chemo will take the rest of his hair. If anyone has seen him lately then you know there's not much left to take. His beautiful eyelashes are falling out now. As we know this is only temporary. Hair grows back. Well, for most of us; right, Kenny?! Whatever hair remains will be lost doing radiation. That's still several weeks away.

RESTING IN HIM

I haven't taken very much time during the updates to talk about how proud I am of my two sons. So today I want to share a few thoughts with you all. I know as mothers we all think we have the best children in the world. And we do. I thank God every day for my two sons. What a blessing they have been to me. Dustan and Dylan are both my heroes.

I think God looks at Dustan and says, "What a faithful servant you are to me. No matter what life has thrown your way you have kept a smile on your face and a joy in your heart."

What an example to me as a mother. So many teenage boys could have said, "Not me! Why me?" and, "I am tired of this—I give up." Not Dustan! He has accepted that this is the plan for his life right now. He gets up every day and says, "Okay, what do you have for me today, Lord?"

He accepts God's answer with a smile on his face.

Dustan is faithful, loving, kind, handsome, smart, and so very wise. Oh, I could go on forever. I just want everyone to see him as I see him. If you have met Dustan then you know I speak truth.

With the same joy I could go on forever about Dylan. He is preparing to give a great gift to his brother.

I think God looks at Dylan and says, "Your zest for life is exactly what I chose for you. From the moment I created you, I knew your zest for life would be contagious. You would take the abilities I have given you and do great things."

God knew that Dylan would need to be here for his big brother. As soon as he learned Dustan needed a bone marrow donor, with his contagious smile and laughter, he said without a second thought, "I will do whatever it takes." He is

Brotherly Love

about to give his zest for life to Dustan. Oh, what a proud moment as a mother. Words cannot even express the feelings in my heart.

Dylan is giving, loving, handsome, energetic, smart, and, yes, oh so funny. One of the most important traits of Dylan's is his love for life. Now he chooses to give this to his brother.

As tears run down my cheeks all I can do is stand in awe of God. For our family to go through such times, and still find God is in the small details? He continues to amaze me.

Oh, what a mighty God we serve. The scripture He gave me today was Joel 2:25, "And I will restore to you the years that the locusts have eaten, the cankerworm, and the caterpillar." I truly believe the Lord will restore back to our family the years this cancer has tried to take from us. As in Job 42:12, "The Lord blessed the latter part of Job's life more than the first." As a family we stand on these scriptures and know that God will restore and bless our lives in His timing.

Please be in prayer with us for each person who fights the battle of cancer: for each child, and the families that battle with them. My heart aches for each. We serve a God Who is able _____! You fill in the blank. No matter what you write in the blank, HE IS ABLE!!!

I cannot write this update and not give God glory and the praise He deserves. We may be in a very small hospital room but there is enough room for Him to share it with us. Every day I see Him in the smallest of details. I thank Him continuously for His love, for without it where would we all be? We would be lost and without HOPE.

There are so many people here and I often wonder what they are thinking. Are they thanking God for where they are, or are they wringing their hands as to why they are here? As we pass in the hallways we all smile and say the polite hello. I know we

RESTING IN HIM

all are thinking the same thing: God, have mercy on my child. *We all have the same gut-wrenching feelings as we watch each child, with a smile on his face, battle this dreadful disease. Even though we are not all lifelong friends we will have a bond like no other. Even the language barrier does not stop our bond. We can look into each other's eyes and see into the heart and know exactly how each feels.*

As I watch the new patients start their journey, the patients like us still on our journey, or the patients who have completed their journey, we have one thing in common: the HOPE that our child will be the one to conquer this disease. As God's word says, we are all brothers and sisters in Christ, we are of the same family. If we cannot feel someone's joy, happiness, pain, grief, sorrow, or struggles, how can we truly say we belong to the same family? This is something I ask myself daily. Do I live within my own small world or do I feel the emotions of others?

Today I feel the emotions of others. I feel their struggles and heartaches. The Lord often wakes me up at night to pray for these dear ones. Is this my purpose right now? This is my purpose always and I will just continue to be obedient to His word and follow the path He has laid for me. I don't think this would have been the one I would have chosen, but I serve a God Who knows all things.

We continue to praise Him with hands raised. I hope each of you will join us.

> *I can get more out of God by believing Him for one minute than by shouting at Him all night.*
> —SMITH WIGGLESWORTH

Resting in Him, April

"Love one another with brotherly affection [as members of one family], giving precedence *and* showing honor to one another" (Romans 12:10, AMPC).

Brotherly Love

This is a beautiful description of brotherly love. For our family, brotherly love truly was a constant. We believed in putting others before ourselves; Dustan especially believed it. He always took the high road in all circumstances. So when the tables had turned, and Dylan could step up and return this love to show honor to his brother, he was all in. He finally felt as if he could make a difference.

For a senior paper on poetry, Dustan wrote about love as a response to the line, "When bless'd with a sense of his love."

LOVE

Love: the word has so many meanings to it. People say it all the time to their family members, girlfriends or boyfriends, and even close friends. To me, the phrase "I love you" is used so lightly, if people only knew how strong that the word really is they would be careful with it. I mean it's used so lightly that when a couple goes out just a few times they're already saying it to each other, and it's always teenagers.

The love I really want to talk about is called brotherly love, because I have experienced that love more than any other love. When I found out that I was diagnosed with leukemia, my brother, Dylan, would never come visit me in the hospital, and he would not even come to my clinic visits with me. So one day I asked him, "What's wrong?"

He told me, "I just don't like seeing you like that, knowing I can't do anything to help. I just feel useless." I understood what he was saying so I just left it alone.

After about two years, the leukemia came back and the doctor said that this time around I would have to have a bone marrow transplant. The doctors tested my mom and dad to see if they could donate their bone marrow to me. The results came back, and they were negative. After hearing that, Dylan stood up from his seat and said to the doctor, "I will donate. Test me!"

RESTING IN HIM

I told Dylan, "Dylan you don't have to do this, because this is not going to be easy. This means surgery for you, and maybe a little pain."

He said, "I don't care. Finally, I have a chance to help you; because for the past couple of years, I have just felt useless. So let me do this." When my brother said that, I really felt the love in the room.

When Dylan was waiting on the results, he was so nervous, because he really wanted it. The next week the results were in. Dylan was a one hundred percent positive match. When he heard this he was so excited, because he told me that he was praying to God all week to let it be a positive match. Dylan really wanted to help me, and I felt that.

Today, because of brotherly love, Dylan went through a four-hour surgery and donated his bone marrow to me. Now I sit here cancer-free all because of a brother who did not like seeing his brother suffer. Dylan likes to joke about the bone marrow transplant. The doctor said that now I will have Dylan's blood running through my veins. So Dylan always says that I'm going to start acting like him or get his curly afro hair. Everybody always laughs about that, because I'm not used to curly hair, especially the afro.

All joking aside, brotherly love is the best love I have ever felt; and because of it, I will now live a normal life. Thanks to Dylan.

The week prior to transplant was a whirlwind. It was physically and emotionally exhausting. We made it through only by God's strength. There were long days still ahead for us, but we knew God would continue to be faithful and walk the journey with us. Even after the long week of treatments and radiation, it was so amazing to see the effect Dustan had on everyone he met. During radiation all the nurses would comment about his smile and his positive attitude. They all would hug on him and tell him everything would be just fine.

Brotherly Love

Every day we would go to the hospital twice; and Dustan was so tired, yet he always had a smile on his face and a kind word to say to everyone. Isn't that how we are all supposed to be? No matter what our circumstance, we are to show the love of God through our actions and kindness. I saw that with my own eyes through my own son. I saw his eyes sparkle with a love that is indescribable. Even though his body was saying no, his heart and spirit were saying yes. What a testimony! Some days I still wonder if he was truly my son. Where did he get such courage and determination? I know he was a gift from God to me and to the world.

He thought the world of his brother and his family. He always put others first. The love he shared was truly the love of his heavenly Father. He demonstrated the act of brotherly love on a daily basis.

My journal entry:
Today is Thursday, 2/21/08. These are my thoughts for today. Scripture, Job 8:21 (NIV), "God will yet fill your mouth with laughter and your lips with shouts of joy."

It has been a very long week. Monday was our rest day from radiation and chemo. Tuesday was transplant day. (I will talk more about that later.) Wednesday was recovery day for our family. Today is Thursday and I am now just settling into the hospital routine and actually feeling like I can move forward.

Monday was a great day. We all had such great anticipation of the transplant day. It was kind of like Christmas when you work and prepare so much for that one special day. You are so excited about that special gift that you can give or get. Dylan was starting to feel a little nervous, but it really did not hit him until the morning of transplant. Dustan and I waited in the hospital, and Dylan with Kenny at home. We were all trying to mentally prepare ourselves for what Tuesday would be like. I did not sleep very well. I knew I would need to meet Kenny and Dylan on the third floor for the surgery preparation at 6:00 a.m. I was afraid I would

RESTING IN HIM

oversleep. Just the thought that Dylan would be in surgery and Dustan would be waiting in his hospital room was more than I could think about.

Tuesday was a very exhausting day, physically, spiritually, and emotionally. Kenny and I waited with Dylan for the procedure to start. Dylan, of course, iPod in hand, did not seem to know anyone was there. I know he was trying to focus on something other than the waiting room. When they called his name we all walked slowly as if we thought we could change time in some way. Dylan still had his sense of humor; as they weighed him he talked about how heavy he was since he had his phone and iPod in his pocket. When we got to the waiting area where they do the i.v. and go over all the details of the surgery, Dylan realized this was it. They asked him to change into the beautiful hospital gown. Of course, that was a joke in itself. When he realized that would be the only thing he was wearing the jokes started. He was so nervous when they did the i.v. that his vein blew. So they had to stick him twice. What a trooper; he never said a word.

The funniest moments were when they gave him medicine to prepare him for surgery. The nurse said, "This will take about fifteen seconds." Well, almost in fifteen seconds Dylan started laughing and feeling really happy. Kenny and I started asking Dylan questions. You know, this medicine is truth serum. Dylan did start saying things I am not sure he would want anyone to know. Another nurse came to tell Dylan some more details. When she walked off he looked at me and said, "Mom, she was pretty, wasn't she?" You see, Dylan had to remove his contacts, so he could not see very well. Okay, well enough to see that a pretty nurse had just talked with him. That is just like Dylan.

Then came the moment. The moment we had been waiting for so long. This was it. We said our goodbyes to Dylan, and off he went rolling down the hall. As Kenny and I walked back to the waiting room we realized now it is in God's hands. We had no control over anything. As if we did anyway. We put Dylan in God's hands and started our process of hurrying up and waiting.

Brotherly Love

In the waiting room were several family members who were going to wait with us. The surgery was to take about an hour and half. After an hour and a half had passed we were getting a little anxious. Then about two hours after they had begun, one of the transplant team came to us and said they were about three-fourths done. Dylan was being stingy with his bone marrow. They were getting as much as they would need but it was taking much longer than they had anticipated.

So off she went, back to the surgery room, as we again were forced to wait. I have to be honest and say I never had thoughts of fear. I knew God was in control of that surgery. I also knew family, friends, classmates, and people we did not even know were praying for both of our sons. So fear was not in my thought process—only victory, victory of new life for Dustan.

Finally, three hours later, the doctor came to give us the news. The procedure was a success. They had gotten three bags of bone marrow. They even brought it out for us to see before it was rushed next door to be processed for Dustan to receive later in the day. I was excited that everything was coming to a close for Dylan. That was what I thought.

I went into the recovery room, and then realized Dylan had gone through a very tough procedure. When I looked at him there in the bed, his lips, cheeks, and eyes were very swollen. He was still waking up from the anesthesia. So he was a little groggy. Although, he knew his mom was there. He reached out for my hand.

When I grabbed his hand, I think everything from the past four months came rushing to my heart. I started feeling very ill. Kenny said I turned white as the sheets on the bed. I asked the nurse for the restroom. Once I got in the restroom I just fell to my knees not knowing whether I was going to throw up or pass out.

I did not realize it, but I had locked the door behind me. So the nurses and Kenny were banging on the door. I just prayed, "Lord, I cannot be sick. My boys need me

RESTING IN HIM

today. Please give me the strength I need." By that time I heard Kenny at the door. I opened the door and there stood a nurse with apple juice. I assured her I was okay. I do not think she believed me. I walked back to Dylan's bed, which was right by the bathroom. They kept giving me apple juice and peanut butter crackers. After a while I got myself back together. I again stood by Dylan's bed and he grabbed my hand stroked it with his fingers and said, oh so sweetly, "I love you."

I looked up at him and said, "You know I am your mom, right?" I thought maybe he was still under the anesthesia and he thought I was his girlfriend. He assured me he knew who I was, his mom. As I looked down at him in the bed I realized I was looking at a very brave man, not a boy. My heart was so full of love and appreciation. Love for Dylan, and for my heavenly Father for giving Dylan to me. Appreciation that my heavenly Father thought enough of me to give me two sons who would change each other's lives forever.

As Dylan waited in recovery, Dustan was getting ready for his transplant. Dustan called and said, "It is time. They are ready to begin." So we left Dylan in the company of family members, and off we went to Dustan's room.

By the time we got there the nurses were starting the bone marrow transfusion. For Dustan, his part was simple. He just had to be hooked up to an i.v., which is what he is used to anyway. So as the nurses began the i.v. drip, other Vanderbilt employees started coming into his room. Vanderbilt realizes just as we do that this day is Dustan's new life day. So they had him a birthday party with presents. I do not think they know the depth of this day as we do. We realized that this is the day the Lord has made and we will rejoice in it. This is the beginning of Dustan's new life.

Whatever obstacles occurred that day, we faced them and went on about our day. After Dylan was released about 5:30 p.m., we wheeled him up to see Dustan. They joked about the day and then we took a family picture. We were all exhausted.

Brotherly Love

Kenny and Dylan went home to rest. Dustan and I fell into our usual spots in the hospital room. Rest is not what I think we got, although we tried.

Wednesday was a day I am not sure how to explain. Emotionally I felt deflated. Everything we had waited for the last four months now was over. The hard work was about to start; well, for Dustan anyway. We had already made up our minds that we would move forward speedily. So we covered Dustan in prayer.

Bone marrow transplant day, February 22, 2008. Right after Dylan's surgery.

RESTING IN HIM

Dylan wrote this poem for Dustan:

To My Brother

*The day I found out that you were sick
Is definitely something I'd never pick!
It made me feel sad, and hurt, too;
But that's nothing compared to what you're going through.*

*You're strong, I know you can get through this,
But I do and will forever miss
Seeing you at home every day,
Watching you shoot basketball and play.*

*You are still young, only seventeen.
Why has this happened? It is not in our genes.
But I know in time you will recover
And do all this stuff, coz you're my brother.*

*I love you so much,
And it hurts to touch—
I know you are in pain
And that it drives you insane.*

*These memories I treasure deep in my heart,
And nothing and no one can pull us apart;
Like the times when we're watching t.v.,
Some funny thing happens, and you look straight at me.*

*I know you sometimes find it hurts to laugh,
But what you can do now is just enough
To make me feel happy and special inside,
Instead of being snappy and trying to hide.*

*Whenever you need my help I'm there,
And I hope you know I truly care.
So keep it up, you're doing great.
And don't worry, I won't eat all the cake.*

Brotherly Love

Brotherly love starts in the heart and then is seen in your everyday actions towards others. For our story, brotherly love started within our own family. Miraculously, we began to see this brotherly love amongst our community. From the moment of Dustan's diagnosis until months after his death we were covered by love. We had a community of people that supported us emotionally, spiritually, and financially.

Dustan's school, Mount Juliet Christian Academy, rallied around us and poured love on us daily. As transplant day was coming up they designed and sold a "Beat Cancer" t-shirt in Dustan's favorite color, RED. Every student, teacher, and faculty member purchased this t-shirt and wore it on the day of transplant in support of our family.

I knew on transplant day, February 19, 2008, MJCA was gathering together in their t-shirts praying over my boys and our family. This picture exemplifies brotherly love:

The power of Dylan's love for Dustan became a place of testing, when, after all this, he ultimately had to face his bitter loss. After all he gave, he still had to take the death of his brother.

RESTING IN HIM

What happens when the one who has taught you so much about the love of a brother vanishes from your life? What do you do with the hole that is left in your still half-beating heart? What emotions surface when your emotional twin is ripped from your existence? How do you pick up the pieces of a broken heart and move forward? When Dylan ultimately lost Dustan, then came the soul-searching. His loss took him in and out of the valleys. Some of the bitterness and finally the victory he gained are shown in one of his poems:

Tu Me Manques
French for "I miss you," but it translates literally, "You are missing from me."

My heart is broken, I do not know why. I sit here toking, as I begin to cry. The tears roll down my face, burning as they leave my eyes.

I can only imagine. I can only imagine what you felt on that night. Pain. In the deepest moments of life, pain is the reminder that we are still living.

Well, I wish I could never be reminded of it again. It plays in my head like a broken record handed down from Mom that quit working five years ago; but I still put it on play, hoping to hear the voice that lullabies my nights into sweet dreams. Until a voice that claimed to be true spoke blasphemy over my dreams, and handed me nightmares instead.

I see you in everything that I do, but how can that be true when I know that you are dead? Your body lays in the grave while I hold this gun to my head ready to see my sweet Savior. And three days later be ready to take the stitches out of my throat from where I try to hang myself on the lies that he told me.

He sold me into fantasies that tasted so sweet, until I saw her plan of deceit. But I wish that I can see—you. I may be clean now but I can't see your smile, and I am having a real hard time determining which is better. I pray that I make the right choice.

Brotherly Love

Either I believe what people have told me, that God took you to teach me a lesson— and if that is true, then you can tell God that I'm better off without him, because I am my own best teacher. I have been giving myself the same lesson since the beginning of creation: I AM NOTHING WITHOUT GOD, and you can see that in my life's work.

Or I can choose to believe that my God is NOT a car-wrecking, cancer-causing Creator, that He is a loving, life-giving Lord. And I choose the latter, I choose the ladder that He stands on reaching down to help me with every step.

All who follow his precepts have a good understanding, that was written in Psalms. Tu Me Manques is written in my palms. To remind myself every time I try life with my own hands, my strength will never suffice.

And just so you know, Mom misses you and Dad does, too. I'm trying not to cry while writing this, but trying not to cry while thinking of you is like trying to think of a reason why Jesus died for us. And to put it in better perspective, why He died for you.

Because you are not alone any more, the very reason that He died is holding you tight in His light. You are His light. We are His life, and His love is the line that strings us to His very presence. So when I feel His love, in essence, I feel you. And my heart holds a special drum solo just for you.

It's funny, looking back five years ago, during our conversations about God I looked into your eyes and I could see heaven; but who knew that was foreshadowing for a life that you are now living?

That pretty much sums up the road Dylan traveled the years after his brother's passing. It was a precarious road. Even in mine and Kenny's own grief we purposely wrapped Dylan up with our love and support. We did not want him to get lost in the shadows of our grief. Yet somehow he got lost in his own.

RESTING IN HIM

As parents you want the best for your children. You pray over them and release them into God's hand for His protection. If you truly know that your Father loves you, then trust is not an issue. I struggled with this on so many occasions, and, honestly, still do. As Dylan's mother I wanted to take his grief from him. It tore at my heart to watch him struggle and deal with his best friend being gone.

When the boys were young a more experienced mother told me, "Now you know how it feels to have your heart live outside your body." I did not get the full impact of that statement until I saw and experienced the intensity of both my boys' pain.

Dylan wrote this around the seventh anniversary of Dustan's passing:

I can remember your face. Even if I never saw another photo of you, I will always remember your face. I can remember your smile, the way you would sit with your arms folded against your stomach. I can remember the way you talked about Mom and Dad and how you were going to buy them a house next to you and your future family and always take care of them. I remember the way you shot a basketball, the way you played the drums, even what your fingers would do when you would sing. If I can remember all those random things then why can I not remember the one thing that I want to remember, your laugh?

I would trade all those things just to hear your laugh. You were always so full of joy. Even during everything that you were forced to go through you were still full of joy. In your sickness you showed me God's grace. It's only seven years later I realized that. In the midst of everything I was angry. Angry at the world, angry at the reason why, but, most importantly and unfortunately, I was so angry at God. Through your sickness I found God's love, but through the understanding of your healing I'm constantly receiving God's grace. When we were kids you loved me with a passion, and now that I'm grown and you're no longer here, I'm able to take the passion that you loved me with and love the world that I once hated—and, most importantly, love the God I once hated.

Brotherly Love

People tell me all the time that they are sorry about you and your death. I was, too, at first, but now I'm not. I'm not sorry, although I'm not thankful either. But I'm not sorry, because through your life I received a certain love that can't be received or ever felt again, and through your death I learned to live with the very passion that you loved me with.

Funny how we all thought that Dylan was giving life to his brother on that famous transplant day in 2008. In reality, Dustan gave life to Dylan.

He taught him how to LOVE. Even through Dustan's death he has given me, Kenny, and Dylan the ability to love God more deeply and people more passionately.

Somewhere Dylan saw the following quote, which summed up his feelings exactly: "True love is when you become a better person just by being in the presence of that other person."

After years of struggling with his brother's death, Dylan was finally able to see some good that had come from not only his brother's struggles but his own. In Dylan's words:

> My brother was a fighter. No matter what came his way during life he fought through it with everything he had. I am so honored to have lived with him and to have been his brother for sixteen years. He taught me so much about fighting for what you believe in and enjoying the time you have on this earth.
>
> When my brother and I were young he was a very competitive person. When we played sports he just always had to be the winner and he would get there no matter what it took. I remember when we were on the same soccer team he would always get the

ball by knocking the other kids down and then passing to me and I would score. We were such a great team. Even if we lost he would always tell me, "Dylan, there is nothing to be sad about. You played a great game; and remember, you learn more from a loss than a win." No matter what we did together he always taught me something valuable about life, even in a lousy soccer game.

My brother enjoyed his life with every moment he could. He could be having the worst day of his life but you sure wouldn't know it. Because he always had this smile on his face and he was always encouraging others, even when he was down.

I remember asking him one day, even through the disasters of life how can you still be putting on a smile and telling everyone who asks you're great. And his reply was, "How can I not be happy? Look what God has given me, a perfect family and great friends. Yeah, we all have bad days, but I know who is taking care of me and guiding every step I take, and that's all I need to know."

He always knew how to answer to the struggles in his life.

My brother went through an enormous trial the last three and a half years of his life with the battle against leukemia. Yet somehow, some way, he still had a smile on his face most of the time, and fought so hard against the devil and this disease.
During those three and a half years he taught me so many things about life. Like even through the valleys of life, God is still there with you, even if you think He has left you. No matter what life throws at you, you stand there like a brick wall and just let it bounce right off you, because the power of God is amazing and He can do anything.

Brotherly Love

What he taught me the most was how precious life is. Don't take anybody or anything for granted, and enjoy the people God gave you on this earth. He put you where you are for a reason, and don't let anybody tell you otherwise.

He taught me all this within sixteen years; just imagine if he was able to live until he was sixty. My brother was an amazing person with a lot of wisdom for an eighteen-year-old. I thank God for giving me the privilege to have been his brother. I thank God for everything my brother taught me. He even got me on the right track with my life. I love you, Bubba.

Summer 1996

CHAPTER 6

Miracles Seen and Unseen

*Miracles happen every day,
change your perception of what a miracle is
and you'll see them all around you.*
—JON BON JOVI

God reminded me today about the small details. I can list many times God has showed up and taken care of the small things for me. God's miracles can happen in big ways; they have, and still continue to do so. But, what I love the most is the miracles in the small details. He just reminds me that He is a personal God and that He knows me by name and continues to take care of all my small details. If I can only open my eyes to see where He is instead of looking at what I think He should be doing. I must be still and stay open-minded so I do not miss the miracles in the small things.

My God remembers me personally and loves to remind me that He is indeed my caring Father. As I search out new scriptures, read devotions, or look over other scriptures so dear to me, I then realize this is my Father's way of leaving small reminders of His

RESTING IN HIM

love throughout my day. If someone I loved left me a love letter but I never picked it up and read it, how would I know how much they loved me? Such as, the word of God. If I do not pick it up and read it, how will I know He loves me and cares for me?

God's word is a MIRACLE, yet to be seen by so many!

Dustan was preparing for graduation and improving every day. He was doing so well the doctors decided to do his hundred-day workup (post transplant) on day eight-four. We were all so excited. We had talked about getting his Hickman line* removed; we talked about his plans up to graduation and all the things he would be able to do afterwards. He was really starting to enjoy life again. We all were.

Then...

On Friday afternoon, May 9, 2008, after the bone marrow test, a call from the doctor. My thoughts as written in my journal:

My phone was ringing and as I ran through the house my thoughts went to Kenny and Dylan. They must be having a great time with Dylan's truck. Then when I saw the number on my phone a lump came into my throat. Why would the doctor be calling me on a Friday afternoon?

When I answered and I heard the voice on the other end my heart stopped. The doctor said, "We received the test back from the bone marrow, and looks like the leukemia is back. It is not in any of his bloodwork, just the bone marrow test."

There were those words again. What?! My heart screamed but my mouth could not say a thing. I just listened as he talked about the results of the test. As I was wondering what to say, this all too familiar feeling was starting to choke me. Literally, I could not say a word and the doctor did not even wait for a response.

*A line placed intravenously for use in administering medications

Miracles Seen and Unseen

He told me he would see us Monday morning in the clinic and hung up the phone.

There I was with this horrible news and no one to tell. Kenny and Dylan had gone out to drive Dylan's truck he had just gotten. It was a five-speed and he was learning how to drive it on the open roads. It was their little adventure for the day. Dustan was upstairs in the movie room with several friends. Oh, God! I am alone with this news. What now?

I just sat in silence. I could not even cry. I was in shock. This cannot be true! Not again! God had promised us that Dustan was going to be okay. The bone marrow transplant had gone so smoothly— just as God promised. Speedily your health will spring forth *was the scripture we all hung on to, and speedily he had made it through this part. NOW—what's this? It must be a mistake.*

As I sat and prayed I felt a peace that I cannot explain come over me, "peace that surpasses all understanding." I just knew God's promise was that Dustan was healed.

So I just prayed with my face to the floor. Then I picked up the phone and called Kenny. I could hear in his voice the fun they were having, and I just could not bring myself to tell him the news I just received. I decided to wait.

I lay on the floor again crying out to God for direction and wisdom. He says: for those who seek will find. I needed to find an answer, I needed to find direction, I needed everything.

Distraught and humbled before the Lord—I was not prepared when Kenny walked in the door. I looked at him and said, "The doctor called."

"And?" he said.

"They say it's back."

RESTING IN HIM

Kenny fell to the floor and broke down. How can I console him when I myself am falling apart? We just sat there crying together and holding each other. We knew we had to once again share the news with the boys and this would send our family into another whirl on the Ugly Monster ride. Kenny and I prayed whether we should tell them now or wait until after the weekend. We knew the hospital was running additional tests. And we just knew this was a mistake. We kept repeating to ourselves and each other, this is a mistake. Why get everyone upset if the news was not true, right?

That's what I want to do. I just want to stay in complete denial and forget this is happening. This is Mother's Day weekend and so many activities are coming up for graduation. We could pretend; or could we?

Does this sound familiar? Have I not already described this scene in another chapter? Exactly! I was living this nightmare again. I remember thinking, *Oh God, do you not love me? Surely, if you love me you would not allow this to happen to our family again.* I knew in my heart of hearts He truly did love me. In my flesh, I questioned everything. In my spirit, I questioned nothing. My flesh and spirit were having a knock-down drag-out fight. My flesh was on my left shoulder and my spirit was on my right shoulder. I did say RIGHT shoulder because your spirit is always right. It seemed as if they were screaming to each other and my soul was caught in the middle.

My head was spinning; and my heart, well, let's just say I felt like someone had taken a knife and stabbed directly in the middle and was twisting and turning it with the power of an army. It hurt with every beat. How much can a heart take before it explodes? I was just starting to find out.

We had finally come to a place where we could see the end of the Ugly Monster. This ride had taken us to places we did not want to go and made us stay a whole lot longer than we wanted to stay. We had finally stopped holding our breath and were beginning to slowly breathe in the refreshing air of good health again. Relapse, Relapse, Relapse—how I hate this word. I hated it more than the word cancer.

Miracles Seen and Unseen

Cancer can be cured most of the time. When we first learned that Dustan had leukemia, his chance of recovery was at 90%. Now, with three relapses, we were at less than 10%. The only word that I could think that would trump relapse was MIRACLE. We needed one and we needed it quickly.

"Miracle" means so many different things to so many different people. I am a very deep thinker, although most of the time I see things only as black or white. My heavenly Father is helping me to see things in color and not to overanalyze everything. He knows this keeps me from seeing things from His perspective. Such as miracles. If I am always looking for a miracle in the way I think it should happen then I have missed the true miracle.

Let me just be honest and reveal to you my heart so you can see the truth of what I believed about miracles. I had heard most of my life that Jesus performed miracles in His lifetime. I believed everything that the Bible stated. Then came the true test. Not only did I have to believe miracles that had happened in Bible times, but I had to believe it could happen in my present time. I had experienced what I call miracles in my life. God had healed me from several different sicknesses, healed my heart from a lot of wounds, blessed me with two beautiful sons, and best of all He accepted me into His family. This I considered the best miracle in my life. Then when the word CANCER was introduced to our family, I stood strong with my belief about miracles. I knew Jesus did and could perform miracles, then and now.

My belief system was getting ready to be turned upside down. I was entering into a place of true commitment. There was no turning back. I either believed or didn't. Was I going to see black or white? There was no place for any grey in between. No way to waver or ride the fence. I had to make a decision and stand behind it.

Now making a decision to believe or not to believe can be easy, unless it is a matter of life or death. Then the stakes are much higher, especially when it is not your decision but someone's you love with everything inside you. What am I saying?

RESTING IN HIM

Once again, the Ugly Monster ride had taken another huge turn. This time we were not only turned upside down we were entering into a tunnel of darkness, a narrow space; we not only couldn't see in front of us, but it permitted no movement to the left or right. There were only two choices. Go forward with little or no hope at all, or stop the ride and exit on our own terms. Easy decision, right? Absolutely NOT!

This word, RELAPSE! We knew we were on the path God had directed for us and we had followed every step He led us to. Then why were things not going as planned? I laugh even writing that statement: "going as planned." Had I not learned through this Ugly Monster ride that nothing goes as I plan? Riding this Ugly Monster was not even my plan to begin with and now we were having to play by its rules. We had trusted God through this entire ride; we knew Dustan's illness was not God's plan, and we hung onto our belief that God could and would heal him from this horrible disease.

One of our scriptures from the very beginning of our journey was Romans 4:20, 21 (NIV), "Yet he did not waver through unbelief regarding the promise of God, but was strengthened in his faith and gave glory to God, being fully persuaded that God had power to do what he promised." The question is, what had God promised?

He promised he would restore health to Dustan, and heal his wounds, Jeremiah 30:17. God's word is full of his promises, and I was holding on for dear life to every one of them that I could find. I would read them over and over again until I could quote them from memory. My thought process was, if I could speak them and do everything I knew to do, then our miracle would come to pass. The truth is, I did not have to do anything, but have faith in God's word and believe. And oh, we believed!

We were now at a place in our Ugly Monster ride where we had to make some major decisions. As I stated previously, we had entered a tunnel of complete darkness with room for no lateral movement. The doctors gave us several options, if that is what you what to call them. Option 1, Dustan could be admitted into the hospital, immediately start very aggressive chemotherapy, and prepare for another bone marrow transplant. Option 2, start on chemotherapy pills, and then after graduation go in the hospital and complete Option 1. Option 3, do nothing and die.

Yep, those were their words, "Do nothing and you will die."

So we walked away from the clinic with a lot of questions but no answers. What option would be best for Dustan? What path did God want us to walk? Were we going to choose life or death?

At this time we were less than two weeks from graduation. Dustan had worked so hard these past eight months to be able to graduate with his class. To walk across that stage to receive his diploma had been his only focus for so long. Now this Ugly Monster was trying to keep him from his goal. How does an eighteen year old make a decision with his life on the line? Yes, we were his parents; we had walked, prayed, and advised him throughout this thirty-one month journey. Now the final decision would be his. It was his life and his body that would be altered by the decisions that were made. Kenny and I knew that whatever decision Dustan chose would be our decision also.

Now let me give you some of the details of these three options.

Option 1 would include an extended hospital stay (probably six to eight months), very aggressive medicines that would have serious complications that would keep him from really living: just existing. Survival rate, less than 10%.

Option 2, take oral chemo and play the wait and see game. (Another whirl on the Ugly Monster with no end in sight.) Survival rate, less than 5%.

Option 3, trust God and stand still. Survival rate not established.

Miracle—this is the word that kept going through my mind. Oh, God, we need a miracle. I pleaded, I cried, I yelled, and even sat in complete silence. I mean, God

RESTING IN HIM

knew everything, right?! I had often trusted God throughout my life for miracles. This was different: life or death.

Let me be brutally honest. After all Dustan had been through the last few years, making this decision was very unclear. He had been slung back and forth with some brutal hits from the Ugly Monster. He had had seizures, mini-strokes, crushed bones in his feet, he'd been burned from the inside out, and he'd been placed in a morphine coma for two weeks. The list goes on and on. This Ugly Monster we rode daily was a tough one, and for Dustan it was only going to get to worse. Is that even possible? Yes, it is. After going over all the details of each option with the doctors, we knew no matter which decision Dustan chose it was going to be the hardest part of this ride.

Have you ever heard the saying, You can't judge a man until you have walked a mile in his shoes? Even though I had walked miles beside Dustan I had never really walked in his shoes. My son would never let you know the agony he felt at each turn or flip of the Ugly Monster. He always just smiled and kept walking. Now you know this momma knew when her baby was in pain. My heart could feel it. Even still, I could not feel the intensity of his physical or emotional pain. I could only imagine what it all must feel like. Watching was more than I could bear. Living it would have had to be excruciating.

Beth Moore gives an illustration in her booklet *Discovering God's Purpose for Your Life*. She's talking about giving a name to the current chapter of her life, "Knowing Christ in the Rubble." She says, "I remember going through a season of time of so much change and so much loss that it was like I'd been standing on a nice spacious piece of concrete and God just came in with a jack hammer and unearthed everything around me except that size 7 right under my feet."

I knew exactly what she was talking about. The piece of concrete we were standing on had completely broken away except where all of our feet were planted. She calls this a "Be Still Moment." There is no place to step. So we had to stand firmly and know that He is God. No matter what was crumbling around us, we were standing!

Miracles Seen and Unseen

Well, here we were not so much *riding* the Ugly Monster as dangling from it. Hanging on with all our might, wrapped in our Rope of Hope—Jesus! I had always heard, When in doubt, DON'T.

None of us had peace with any options except No. 3: "BE STILL AND KNOW THAT I AM GOD."

What did this mean for Dustan? What did this mean for our family? We did not know any of these answers. What we did know was God had never failed or forsaken us. We had faith that God would heal Dustan.

"Now faith is the substance of things hoped for, the evidence of things not seen" (Hebrews 11:1, NKJV). Our hope was in God's power to heal, even though we did not see that healing in his body yet. Walking in faith can be tricky. It's really easy to trust and believe when everything is working out the way you want it to be. The trick is to trust and believe when you do not see the result you want. Oh, wait—that is faith.

So, as Beth Moore asks, "What do you do when he's turning up every bit of ground around you except what you're standing on?" Funny I don't even remember any ground under my feet. I do remember his truth.

Here's what we had to stand on:
"You shall not die, but live, and declare the works of the LORD" (Psalm 118:17, NKJV).

"But I will hope continually, and will praise You yet more and more" (Psalm 71:14, NKJV).

"I will wait on the LORD, who hides His face from the house of Jacob; and I will hope in Him" (Isaiah 8:17, NKJV).

"Let us hold fast the confession of *our* hope without wavering, for He who promised *is* faithful" (Hebrews 10:23, NKJV).

"This *hope* we have as an anchor of the soul, both sure and steadfast, and which enters the *Presence* behind the veil" (Hebrews 6:19, NKJV).

"Without faith *it is* impossible to please *him*" (Hebrews 11:6).

"Yet he did not waver through unbelief regarding the promise of God, but was strengthened in his faith and gave glory to God, being fully persuaded that God had power to do what he had promised" (Romans 4:20,21, NIV).

You see, this was our ground we were standing on. We knew God's plan was to heal Dustan. We would not waver! We would not doubt! In a letter to his wife, Oswald Chambers wrote: "Be patient and so utterly confident in God that you never question His ways or your waiting time."

My *Hinds' Feet in High Places* devotional again came at just the right time:

"Have you ever been in a place that felt like 'the valley of the shadow of death,' or stared into a future where all your dreams and hopes appeared to be dashed into a zillion little pieces?"

These words were haunting. We never expect nor ask for such trying times. Although, it is in these moments that our minds must accept God's word rather than our emotions. It's the collision of feelings and facts that causes us to experience a whole new truth: that we must lay down our life for Jesus.

"He who has found his life shall lose it, and he who has lost his life for My sake shall find it" (Matthew 10:39, NASB).

When we experience God working through our own emotions to bring about his truth it becomes less frightening. It is at that moment we can release our emotions to Him and let Him be our strength. He will never leave us or forsake us.

Miracles Seen and Unseen

My voice was authentically in unison with the prayer in the devotional:

"Lord Jesus, my emotions are numb. It seems like You are really requiring too much this time! Nevertheless, I give you my entire being."

The writer had penned my thoughts. How is that possible? How did she know what I was thinking? Had someone else felt this way? Had someone struggled with my same thoughts? Yes and yes! After pondering these words, I knew the answer.

I must surrender my entire being. Not just my own life and expectations, but most importantly, I had to surrender one of my most treasured gifts, my son. Yes, I had to lay my son at Jesus' feet. I had to let go and give him to God.

That's so much easier said than done. I just lay on the ground with my nose to the floor. I cried out to God and reminded Him that He had given me Dustan. I knew He loved Him so much more than I could have ever imagined. I knew He wanted what was best for him and that I would trust Him no matter the outcome. I believe most of us believe in miracles, but the true miracle is being able to give all to God and let His will be done.

Journal entries:

May 23, 2008

I am so amazed at Dustan's faith. What a change since all of this has happened. I mean a one hundred eighty degree turn around. I believe Dustan was leaning on my faith for a long time. Now God has brought him to a place where he had to find his own. He had to know with everything inside him that he is healed. He has to live and walk by his own faith. Praise God—he is walking by his own faith now. What a blessing to watch my son turn into a man of God. Oh, how I love him.

RESTING IN HIM

May 30, 2008
Dustan had a really long, hard day. He just was not feeling a hundred percent. The chemo pills were starting to make him sick and tired again. After dinner Dustan & I talked about our day and how the enemy rages war against our minds. We talked about our faith— especially his faith and how far he had come. He looked at me with those big baby blues and said, "Mom, without you I would not be where I am. I love you!"

Well, my heart just leaped out of my chest. Oh, I love him so much. I told him, "It is not because of me but our faith in God."

He said, "I would not change a thing I have gone through." He said, "I am who I am because of this journey."

Oh, my heart is so proud. Only a mature, spiritual man of God could say that. Only a man after God's own heart can say those words and mean it. Oh, God, give him the desire of his heart. He has followed you and loves you so.

To me, watching my son transformed from a teenager with such fears of the future, to a man who not only knew his heavenly Father, but walked with him every step, trusting him for every breath—that is an unseen miracle to the spectators of our journey. For me as a mother it is a miracle to my eyes.

To walk through the valley of death as this world knows it, yet really seeing the heights of life through Jesus' eyes—this is not a miracle to most, but to our family it was one of the most treasured miracles.

God prepared Dustan for his cancer diagnosis. He knew the moment he felt the lump behind his ear it was cancer. God had given him peace at the moment that everything would be okay. Every time he relapsed, he knew before the doctors confirmed it. Also, God gave Dustan a dream about the seizures he would have, so that he would be prepared and not afraid. He had complete peace that God was with him at all times.

For a young teenage boy, so afraid of the unknowns of life, to become a strong man of faith in so little time; yes, I call that a true miracle.

In Beth Moore's *Believing God* she makes the statement, "God's eyes are fastened with eternal intentions on the inner man. That's why sometimes God may prioritize performing a miracle on our hearts and minds over a miracle concerning our circumstances."

Later she adds, "Thankfully, God can often perform a miracle in our circumstances and in our hearts and minds simultaneously."

I had already seen God perform miracles in our hearts and minds; NOW I needed Him to perform one in our circumstance.

Oh, Ugly Monster, you will not control this ride. There is someone else at the controls. There is a reason why our problems are called a "circumstance," because when your *circum* (things that take shape around you) comes your way, the outcome all depends on your *stance* (the way you stand against your problems). We are standing! This ride is over!

When I read Hebrews 4:15,16 (NKJV) about Jesus sympathizing with our weaknesses, "For we do not have a High Priest who cannot sympathize with our weaknesses, but was in all *points* tempted as *we are, yet* without sin. Let us therefore come boldly to the throne of grace, that we may obtain mercy and find grace to help in time of need," I believe Jesus had felt this mother's heart.

He knew my heart and head needed to line up with His truth. What was the truth? His word, His promises, HIM! All we had was Jesus and all we needed was Jesus!!!

Dustan, one year old, May 1991

He had discovered his love for the drums, spring 1993

Freshman year of MJCA, marching band, fall of 2004

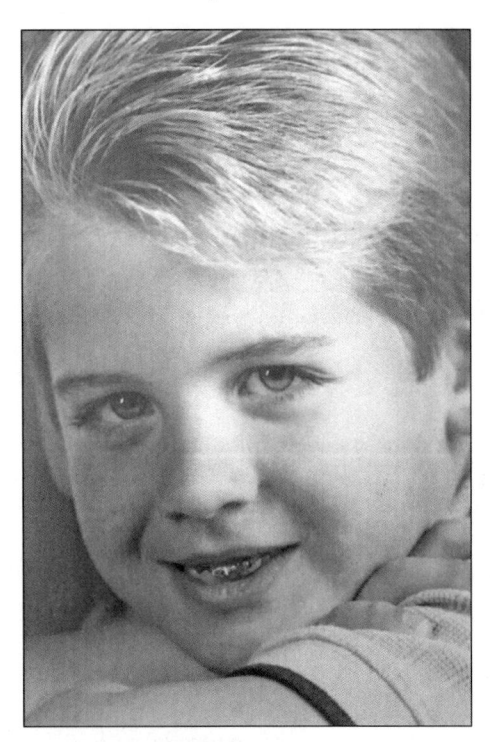

Modeling, LifeWay catalog, fall of 1999

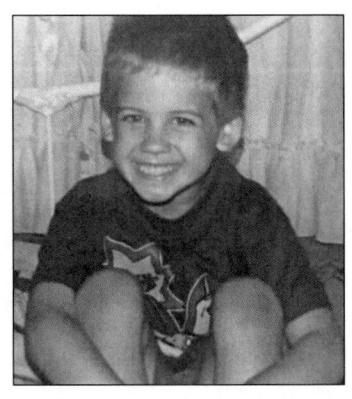

His beautiful smile, summer 1994

Dustan and Dylan modeling, LifeWay children's catalog, fall of 1999

Fall of 2002, "My Sweet Boys"

MJCA basketball season 2007, Dustan assistant coach, Dylan player

Family beach vacation, Grayton Beach, Fla., summer 2006

The boys' last photo together, Dustan's graduation, May 30, 2008

CHAPTER 7

What Was, What Is, What Will Be

*Jesus said to her,
'I am the resurrection, and the life;
he who believes in Me will live even if he dies,
and everyone who lives and believes in Me
will never die.'*
(JOHN 11:25,26, NASB)

Dear Prayer Partners,
Day 69 and counting, post-transplant.
Just a quick update on Dustan and his progress. Last week went really well. His two doctor appointments were very quick. This is a good thing! They said he looks good and everything is going on schedule. His appetite is getting better, as well as his strength. He is a work in progress.

RESTING IN HIM

For those who have not seen him, he looks fabulous. His hair is coming back quickly. It looks blonde, but who knows. It is still too early to know whether it will be curly (like Dylan's) or not. Dustan jokes and says if it is he will shave his head. Whether curly or straight I am glad he is finally getting hair. After losing almost forty pounds and having his hair back, he looks like a different person. You will always be able to recognize his amazing smile. Glad that is back, too!

Saturday was the Junior-Senior Formal for the school. Dylan was asked by his friend to attend with her. This is also when the seniors do their walk. Since Dustan could not attend he decided for Dylan to do his walk with me as my escort—very emotional to say the least. The night was perfect. Everyone looked amazing.

When they announced Dustan's name, Dylan and I had to meet in the middle. I thought I was going to lose it. I worked really hard not to cry. You see, if I did start I would not be able to stop. That would not have been a pretty sight. ☺ As we stood there and listened to the narrator read Dustan's words about his past high school experiences and his future plans it was bittersweet. I know so many parents (Vanderbilt Children's Hospital parents) that would have given anything for their children to experience that joy. Even though Dustan was not physically present I know that he will be able to experience his future plans. So I continuously give God all the glory for what he has done and for what he will do!!!!

"I know the thoughts that I think toward you,...thoughts of peace and not of evil, to give you a future and a hope" (Jeremiah 29:11, NKJV).

This scripture has been engraved upon my heart. Though God knows our future, I know it may not be the future we have envisioned for ourselves. That is where my peace comes from: knowing that the future He gives is the only future I desire. I also desire this for my family, that they too will embrace the future God has for them.

What Was, What Is, What Will Be

This has been a difficult week; Dustan will not enjoy the last few weeks of school as other seniors. Although, he knows firsthand that the next chapter in his life is truly getting ready to begin. His words that were read Saturday night continue to ring in my heart: "Enjoy each day because you do not know when it could be taken from you." These are words of wisdom that can only be felt when they have been lived.

I want to thank each of you for the very encouraging words that we have received this week. You will never know how much this has meant to me, Kenny, Dustan, and Dylan. Your continued support is appreciated and much needed in the days ahead. Even though we are almost to the hundred-day mark, Dustan's journey will continue a lifetime.

I will continue to update.

Resting in Him on My Knees, April

Today I am thankful that I have today. I pray I will accomplish what the Lord has planned for me.

How can things change so quickly? It's the same as on a roller-coaster; you have no idea when the ride will go from enjoyable to unpleasant. The squeal of excitement reaching the top of that long climb and ready for the BIG descend suddenly turns to a heart-wrenching deep groan. You know, the one that sounds like fingernails across a chalkboard. Our family was holding our ears to escape this deafening sound. The sound of life breaking in a million pieces because we could not hold on any more. We had to let go of everything. We had to let go of what was, what is, and what will be.

Throughout our entire journey we never lost hope. We never gave up. We never doubted Dustan would be healed. We stood on every promise in the Bible. We were meticulous about what we believed, the words we said, and the steps we took. Every single detail in our lives was prayed over, even to the smallest of details and decisions. We felt as a family we could not afford to make any mistakes. It's funny now when I go back and read my daily writings. I can see God's handprint on every word. At the time they were my words, my praises, my groans and complaints. Now every word, sentence, and paragraph forms a story: our story—our lives lived out on paper.

Now is the time, God says. *It is time I bring Dustan home. It's time, April.* Those words bring me comfort today. Not so much the first time I heard them. I cried out to God with a quiet but stern, *NO! NO! NO! You promised he would be okay. You promised to take care of him. I am not listening! I know this is not You, God!*

How many times in our lives do we put our hands over our ears and say, NO! I am not listening! We do not listen because we are afraid to do what God is asking of us. I am reminded of a small child who puts his hands over his ears and mutters so he cannot hear what his parents are saying. Children and adults alike play this game to keep from hearing what to them is unpleasant.

I was in my prayer time, facedown on my bedroom floor—pleading and reminding God he had promised that Dustan would be healed, reciting His word back to Him: "I shall not die, but live, and declare the works of the Lord" (Psalm 118:17, NKJV). "Yet he did not waver through unbelief regarding the promise of God, but was strengthened in his faith and gave glory to God, being fully persuaded that God had power to do what he had promised" (Romans 4:20,21, NIV). What had God promised me?

From the day Dustan was born he was a gift from God. He was a beautiful, healthy baby boy with big blue eyes and a smile that could melt the hardest heart. Growing up he was shy, quiet, and very compliant. He never pretended to be anything or anyone he was not. Everything he tried he would succeed at. He may not have been the best or the one in the spotlight, but he never gave up. He gave everything he had to everything he attempted. Cancer was no exception.

What Was, What Is, What Will Be

So when the doctors outlined Dustan's options, it was a decision made with prayer, God's word, his direction, and our complete surrender. It was not a decision made easily or quickly. Looking back, it was almost as if the decision were made for us. Every detail of those last few weeks seemed to be perfectly planned out: not as I, a recovering control freak, would have liked.

Still, I don't think I could have planned out anything as perfectly as it had happened.

My thoughts as written in my journal, June 2008:

This has been a week I cannot really explain. Monday when we went to the clinic, Dustan and I knew this was the day for him to tell the doctors his decision. He did not want to return to the hospital and repeat all the treatments again. He would do medicines at home. We were not worried about the doctors' response. We were sure they would say he was giving up. I really did not care what they thought. I just wanted to do what Dustan and God wanted. I knew we were exactly where we were supposed to be. No one could tell us any differently. We had peace that surpassed all understanding.

We got to the clinic. Dustan's doctor came in the room. She asked what his decision was. Dustan boldly said, "I am not going in the hospital." At that moment she went silent.

She said, "Okay, I understand why you do not want to; quality of life is much more important than quantity. If you go in-patient you will be very sick and feel horrible. I cannot tell you how long it would take, or even if this treatment would work. From this point on we would be in experimental mode."

There, she said it! They really did not know what would work or not at this point. There was our answer. We had truly done everything we knew to do medically. Now it was God's turn.

RESTING IN HIM

Our doctor looked at us with tears in her eyes and said, "This would not be my choice for you, but I completely understand. If I knew one hundred percent sure it would cure you, I would encourage you to do the treatment. I cannot promise you anything."

When we left the clinic Dustan, and I knew with confidence this was the path he was to take. We both had such complete peace. On the way home I asked Dustan, if he knew God would not heal him, would he do the hard-core experimental treatment? He said, "Yes, I would do everything the doctors asked me to do." Then he said, "Mom, I have done everything medically I can do. I know God is going to heal me. So I am okay with this path."

I told him, "You know they think you will die." He said, "Yeah, but they are wrong. They will see; and I cannot wait until it happens." He said, "I am not worried about the timing—I just know it WILL HAPPEN!!! I am sure of it."

Oh my! What more could a mother ask for from her children? To see him walk in such surety of faith, to know God's hands are all over him. My heart rejoiced.

Everyone thinks we are crazy! That's okay—in God's word it states that we must separate ourselves from the world. We have. We now are living in the spiritual realm. By human eyes Dustan is going to die. But by spiritual eyes he will be a miracle and he will live and declare the works of the Lord.

Just to sum up the rest of the week, it has been somewhat of a roller-coaster ride. Not that our faith had wavered, but our flesh tried to creep in. Our flesh is just like a weed in the garden. You think you have them under control, and when you least expect it, there it is trying to creep up and take over. We continuously renew our minds with each other, with the word, with music, and with our memories of what God has done in the past.

One morning I looked in the mirror and I saw myself looking back. Is this really happening? I thought. Are we really faced with death? God's peace is so strong

What Was, What Is, What Will Be

sometimes I forget what the doctors are saying or believing. I mean, Dustan is going on with his life. He is going to basketball camp, hanging out with friends, going to church, and really just living. Doing all the things he has missed out on. The doctors do not know this. They think he will be deathly sick. They continue to caution us about infections, fever, and Dustan just feeling bad.

How do I know God is right here in the midst? Dustan feels good. He is already eluding the doctors' symptoms. You see every time we visit the doctors. They ask the same questions: Are you feeling okay? YES, *he answers. Are you hurting anywhere?* No, *he answers. Are you sure?* YES, *absolutely sure. Then the doctor will ask, What were your symptoms the other two times? Dustan would go over the symptoms again:* Bruising, tired, fever, felt awful, and headaches. *They would ask sternly, Now are you sure you do not have any of these? Dustan would say,* NO, I do not!

I really think the doctors suspect we are lying, that we are in denial and we just do not want to tell them the truth. Even though the bloodwork looks really bad, Dustan feels good. There is no denying that.

So as I go over all this in my mind and I look in the mirror again, I ask myself, Why my son? Why must he go through all of this? Then, as the face in the mirror looks back, it says, Why not my son? What makes him any different from any other son? God's plan— God's plan for his life. That makes him different.

God knows what we must go through and why. I don't know the answers to the WHY questions or even the WHEN questions; all I know is the WHO answer: GOD! I trust Him with everything I am or hope to be. I trust Him with myself and my son.

Is that hard to say or do, you ask? Well, a couple of years ago, yes. I honestly do not think I could have said that. I was such a control freak. Sure, I claimed to trust God, and even proclaimed that I trusted God. But, if you had asked me then to be like Abraham and sacrifice my son, I would have said NO!!!! I cannot let go of him. I love him so much.

You see what I had learned in those last two and a half years. God loves my son much more than I do. So if I really love my son as I say I do, then I must release him out of my control and let God be God. YES, the control freak that I was had to give up my son so that God, not I, had the place of authority. Now the question is, do I trust God? That's another lesson I have learned. Who else is there to trust? We had trusted Vanderbilt, the doctors, and ourselves. Where did that get us? Nowhere! All of these had failed.

But remember, God never fails. So why can I trust Him? Because in His word He says He will never leave us nor forsake us. He had proven time and time again these truths. Who else would I trust now? I have to say it had been a very lonely journey. It was just Kenny, Dustan, Dylan, and me — and of course, God!

God sometimes reveals things to me by repetition. On one particular day God had given me the words, "The shadow of death…I fear no evil," Psalm 23; also the image of a chart and path. At times when God gives me these little nuggets I am unsure what the purpose may be. I just pray for wisdom, that God will open my eyes to see and my ears to hear what he is showing me.

The same day, God gave me Ephesians 1:4, "just as he chose us in Christ before the foundation of the world to be holy and blameless before him in love" (NRSV). This is a very powerful verse; but the true power comes when you read it with its entire context.

> Ephesians 1:3–13 (NRSV):
> Blessed be the God and Father of our Lord Jesus Christ, who has blessed us in Christ with every spiritual blessing in the heavenly places, just as he chose us in Christ before the foundation of the world to be holy and

What Was, What Is, What Will Be

blameless before him in love. He destined us for adoption as his children through Jesus Christ, according to the good pleasure of his will, to the praise of his glorious grace that he freely bestowed on us in the Beloved. In him we have redemption through his blood, the forgiveness of our trespasses, according to the riches of his grace that he lavished on us. With all wisdom and insight he has made known to us the mystery of his will, according to his good pleasure that he set forth in Christ, as a plan for the fullness of time, to gather up all things in him, things in heaven and things on earth. In Christ we have also obtained an inheritance, having been destined according to the purpose of him who accomplishes all things according to his counsel and will, so that we, who were the first to set our hope on Christ, might live for the praise of his glory. In him you also, when you had heard the word of truth, the gospel of your salvation, and had believed in him, were marked with the seal of the promised Holy Spirit.

I read these scriptures over and over again; and in time, it started to come together. God chose the redeemed to make Him seen in the world. I believe God was showing me that if our family wanted to walk out our God-given destiny, then on this path we must follow Him like children. Our security comes from Father God; being secure in Him helps us keep our footing. Our stability is knowing we have obtained our inheritance in Christ. He has adopted us in the great family of all the faithful in heaven and on earth; we are accepted in the Beloved. We have to walk in the truth that He chose us before time to stand before Him in love.

Always obey the voice of God.

Follow His word (Spirit) over our emotions (flesh).

Be persistent, as he dictated in Ephesians 6:13 (NIV): "Put on the full armor of God, so that when the day of evil comes, you may be able to stand your ground, and after you have done everything, to stand."

RESTING IN HIM

At times we must take bold action. Once you have received God's direction, act on what He has commissioned you to do, and watch your miracle happen before your eyes.

Only from our new heart can the Spirit-led life flow. There is a threefold purpose to the Spirit-led life. You have been called to walk in love (the cross) just as Christ loved us; to walk in light (His truth), being led not by your own thoughts but the wisdom of God's word; and to walk by faith (heaven), the assurance of things hoped for but yet unseen.

> What Was—The Cross
> What Is—His Truth
> What Will Be—Heaven/Freedom

To walk where you have never been, you need guidance beyond yourself and your natural abilities. Jesus knew that. So He promised to send the Comforter, the Holy Spirit, by His indwelling. He will walk you through everything God has desired you to accomplish. First Thessalonians 2:12 is a prayer "that you would walk worthy of God who calls you into His own kingdom and glory" (NKJV).

Obey, act in faith, stand with persistence, and take bold action. If you look these words up you will find that being obedient is "complying with or being submissive to authority," faith is "belief that is not based on proof," to stand is "to remain firm or steadfast," and taking bold action is "not hesitating or being fearful in the face of actual or possible danger; courageous and daring." This sounds like the definition of the sons and daughters of God. So God was asking us to walk the path of exactly who we were; His children.

As any parent knows, if you encourage your children to believe in who they really are (a Gammon—standing together with our values and our beliefs), then you are standing right alongside them and you've got their backs. God had our back.

What Was, What Is, What Will Be

We believed God for something BIG, something only He could do. We believed Him for a miracle. Not just any miracle but the most important miracle of our lives, Dustan's life. We waited patiently for our circumstances to line up with our promises from God's word. We did not stand still and do nothing. We kept walking forward and living life, knowing our miracle was coming.

The miracle that came looked very different from the one we were expecting.

How is it that this roller-coaster ride has now come to its destination? Somewhere along the way I did not hear the final call. I missed the operator informing me that this ride had come to an end. It had stopped, the lap bars had been released and we were being asked to exit the ride.

Wait! What?! I cannot get off this ride without my son. No, I refuse to leave!! Here we are, Dylan, Kenny, and I, sitting motionless. All these people circled around us watching and waiting. I cannot leave without Dustan. I cannot walk away from this thirty-one month ride without him by my side. Sorry, I refuse to leave!

What happens when the miracle you have longed for and waited so patiently for arrives differently? Everything you believe, everything you stand for, and everything you are comes crashing around your feet. All the scriptures you've read and believed—suddenly, they mean nothing. All these words, thoughts, and feelings come rushing in but you have no idea how to put them together to make sense. You just have to figure out how to breathe.

Breathe.... Breathe. How did I forget how to breathe? Oh God, help me to breathe!

Have you ever been driving somewhere when all of the sudden you look up and don't remember how you got there? That's how it was during Dustan's last days, his visitation, and the celebration of life. We were walking through a fog of denial. *How could this really be happening to us? Are we really saying goodbye to our son? Can Dylan say goodbye to his brother? What are all these people doing here around us? We just need the world to stop. We need everyone to understand that our lives have stopped. We are still feeling sick from the roller-coaster; we cannot possibly be getting on another ride.* Reality hits and we enter into the House of Mirrors.

The basic concept behind a house of mirrors is to be a maze-like puzzle. In addition to the maze, you are also given mirrors as obstacles, and false leads into inaccessible parts of the maze. Sometimes the mirrors may be distorted, to present reflections that may be humorous or frightening.

We did not enter this house on our own volition. We were shoved violently, and the door slammed behind us.

Unlike the roller-coaster ride where we had someone guiding us and instructing us along the way, the house of mirrors had no guide, no direction, and no instructions. You were on your own. Engulfed in darkness, we could not even find our footing. We were used to being a family of four, holding on to each other; and now one of us was missing. We tried to get up. We tried to stand. We just kept falling over. We could not find our balance. This house of mirrors also had an unsteady foundation. The ground beneath us would go up and down without any notice. Oh, we thought the roller-coaster ride was intimidating and frightening. We had no idea the journey that awaited us.

WHAT WAS:
A family of four, living a wonderful, beautiful, messy, imperfect life. Together we knew we had a strong bond and foundation that would last a lifetime. Our values and beliefs, based on the word of God, were strong. An entire family having to reach deep down and hang onto what we said we believed. A fifteen-year-old boy withstanding a trial of his own faith, and all of us watching his faith grow stronger and stronger.

What Was, What Is, What Will Be

WHAT IS:

A family of three, no longer living, but merely existing and looking for any meaning in life. Together we still knew we had a strong bond, even though our foundation had cracked. Our values and beliefs were now being examined and questioned, and our faith now being tested to unbelievable limits. Will we survive this tragic event in our life? Will God's faithfulness prove to be true? Will God's love overcome our pain and doubts? Will we be victims or victors? Will be become bitter or better?

WHAT WILL BE:

A family transformed from darkness to light. A three-corded bond held together by truth, hope, and love. A story that continues to unfold as the hope of Christ shines through us.

What was, what is, what will be—God is the same in all three of these places. He has never and will never change, and neither has His promise or His word. Our perception of Him and His word changed, but never God.

CHAPTER 8

Taking a Step Out of the Boat

*And looking at them Jesus said to them,
'With people this is impossible,
but with God all things are possible.'
(MATTHEW 19:26, NASB)*

*Dear Prayer Partners,
Day 87 and Counting.*

We need your prayers. We received a call from the doctor on Friday afternoon. The news was not good. He told us that Dustan's bone marrow test looked like it has leukemia cells. He was shocked as were the rest of the doctors. This test does not hold true to all the other tests that have been done. All the other tests were perfect. Even his blood work does not show anything. He had us go in today for some more bloodwork. Again, everything came out great. SO the final decision will be based on the donor cell count (remember this is Dylan's cells).

RESTING IN HIM

Last check, Dustan was one hundred percent Dylan. So our family believes that the bone marrow test is a fluke. That the donor cell count will again be one hundred percent. The results of this test will not be back until late tomorrow (Tuesday) afternoon.

I cannot even begin to tell you how this news has devastated our family. We came together Friday as a family and talked, cried, and prayed. We all feel that God is sovereign. He knew before Dustan was born what the test results were going to be Friday. Nothing is a surprise to Him. We laid our fears and doubts at His feet. We have praised Him for Dustan's healing and we continue to praise Him for his healing. We know GOD IS SOVEREIGN and we continue to give HIM ALL THE GLORY!!!!

I asked the doctors if they believed in miracles. They said, "Well...if the donor cell count comes back a hundred percent Dylan, then yes, and we will run the halls with you." Only God can show out now. We trust Him!

If the donor test comes back one hundred percent Dylan's cells then they will do another bone marrow test this week. So we find ourselves in another hurry up and wait situation. What is faith unless you have to put it to action? I can say that our family has put it to action more than once.

God's word is full of his promises and we stand on them all. Yes and amen!!!

"Nothing is impossible with God" (Luke 1:37, NLT).

He can do exceedingly, abundantly more than we ask or think (Ephesians 3:20, NASB).

He is life (Romans 6:23).

"Be anxious for nothing, but in everything by prayer and supplication with thanksgiving let your requests be made known to God. And the peace of God,

Taking a Step Out of the Boat

which surpasses all comprehension, will guard your hearts and yours minds in Christ Jesus" (Philippians 4:6,7).

I could go on and on. As I said, we are standing on His entire word.

I hope you will stand with us in this little hurdle of our journey. Praise God that Dustan is one hundred percent Dylan, and that his journey will continue cancer free. Remember there is POWER IN PRAYER! Not only does it change circumstances, it also changes us through the circumstances.

My devotion today:
"When we make our first reaction to what happens in our lives a reaffirming praise to God for who He is, we invite His presence to inhabit the situation and His power to come and change things. This is the hidden power of praising God." (Stormie Omartian, The Prayer That Changes Everything*)*

I will update tomorrow with the results from the test. A huge thank you to those who continue to hold my arms up when I find I am weary.

On My Face Before Him, April

Today I am thankful God is always sovereign.

After everything our family had been through in the last few years—a cancer diagnosis, stroke, seizures, two relapses, loss of job, financial burdens—you would think we could handle hurdles. No matter how prepared you think you are for life's detours, you never adjust to having your hopes and dreams shattered again. The one thing you had been working so hard to get to/through was pulled from your reach.

I have learned several things on my journey of life. Sometimes God asks you to step out of the boat (to see if you are willing) and other times He asks you to stay in the boat and make room for Him to get in with you. These are the times the water can get rough. Getting out of the boat is a role of boldness and obedience, and staying in the boat is a role of trusting and knowing He is there, regardless of whether you see or feel Him.

Often in times of uncertainty in our lives we do not recognize Jesus. It is in these times complete surrender and trust is necessary.

According to Hebrews 6:19, "This hope we have as an anchor of the soul, both sure and steadfast, and which enters the *Presence* behind the veil" (NKJV). The anchor is what holds you steady. When God directs you to stay in the boat He is the anchor that you can hold onto. No matter how rough the waters or fierce the storm becomes, you can be assured that your boat will not sink.

During the days while we were waiting for the test results to be finalized I would read this scripture over and over. Each time, it would bring hope to my heart. I was thinking, This is just like God to bring this scripture to my remembrance. Every time I would quote it I would have thoughts tumbling throughout my mind; and, trust me, thoughts were constantly tumbling. This image came to my mind: I can see our journey as a boat ride where you start out sailing along not sure what your destination will be. Then, as you sail, your boat starts off a little rough, the waters tossing you to and fro. Your supplies are water, Bible, pen, paper, and just enough food. The waters begin to get extremely rough. You grab hold of each other (Dustan, Dylan, Kenny, and I) and hang on for the journey ahead. Before you know it, the darkness comes upon you. Sometimes the water is tossing you and sometimes the waters are calm. You cannot see the Bible because the darkness is so thick. You pray hard that His word will come flowing back into your mind. As it does the darkness starts to lift. Then you realize as the darkness is lifting the sun is starting to shine through. You grab the word again and start reading as much as you can before the darkness comes again. Then, as quickly as the sun came, darkness falls; but this time you realize you can see a glimpse of your path ahead because of the light of the moon (the word written upon

Taking a Step Out of the Boat

your heart). As you travel this journey day and night, day and night, day and night sometimes you can see others along your path, which gives you the gentle nudge you need or even replenishes your supplies. Then at other times, you realize you and your family are all alone in this boat. At times you can feel the loneliness of the days and nights, and at other times you welcome the calm silence of the journey. There are times you feel the sun on your face and a slight wind brush through your hair. Then you know God is with you. Then the other moments you feel the rain hitting you so hard it feels like a knife cutting your skin. You hear the sound of the thunder and see the lightening, but again you know God is with you. No matter how rough the ride, the boat never sinks and you do not fall out. The anchor holds you firmly.

As Corrie ten Boom describes it, "In order to realize the worth of the anchor, we need to feel the stress of the storms." (*Jesus Is Victor*)

I am a very visual person so I love when God gives me picture images. Words are very powerful, but when I can see the words as a story it comes alive to me. I have always loved mystery movies. To watch the story and try to figure out the details of how, when, why, and who exhilarates me. It is a part of my DNA to analyze and understand all details. God knows this about me and yet he was asking me this time to just trust without any details or answers. Is this considered denial or faith?

Even as I write the above statement, I can already hear some of you saying, "Huh? Denial or faith. What do you mean by that?" Through some very difficult times in my life I have had to ask this same question to myself: Am I denying the truth of my situation or am I standing in faith on God's promises? I have found that there is a fine line between walking by faith and denial.

Walking by faith does not mean that I am denying the truth of my situation, whether it is financial, health, or a test of my true character. What faith means is that I am acknowledging and even speaking aloud what my situation is; but, right after that, I am confessing with my mouth the truth of what God's word says about my situation.

RESTING IN HIM

Now denial is the fear to even speak about my situation—afraid if I speak it, then someone will automatically think I do not have faith in God. You can deny your circumstances, but they are what they are. If you do not speak them aloud and let others hear and see it, then how will anyone know that your faith and your God are bigger than your circumstance?

Okay, here's an example. Let's just say I am feeling sick today. A friend notices and asks me, "You look like you do not feel well." The denial response: "Oh, no, I am just fine" (so that others will not think I am weak in my faith). The faith response: "Not feeling my best, BUT I know I am healed in Jesus' name" (I have stated the fact and then the truth).

I know this is kind of a cheesy example but it still proves my point. You live in denial if you want everyone to think, *Oh, no, I am not sick; I am great*, even though the fact is, you are feeling sickly. You live in faith if you can acknowledge the truth, and know what His word says about your situation.

Let's take a look at Isaiah 43:2: "When you pass through the waters, I will be with you; and through the rivers, they will not overflow you. When you walk through the fire, you will not be scorched, nor shall the flame burn you" (NASB).

What does this verse indicate? When you go through waters, rivers, and fires, He will take care of you. It does not say *if* you go through waters, rivers, and fires. The key word here is "WHEN," which tells me: Be ready, because you will travel through some difficult ways. The awesome part of this verse is, even though I will travel a difficult path I will travel through with Jesus, and He will make sure I am not harmed in the process.

I have done some research to see if at any time we are not to acknowledge our circumstances. I have not found one time in the Bible that says not to speak of what you are going through. On the contrary, our goal in life is to magnify, proclaim, and

Taking a Step Out of the Boat

live out Christ before the world. How do we do this if in fact we do not speak of the difficulties we are walking through?

"For I am well assured and indeed know that through your prayers and a bountiful supply of the Spirit of Jesus Christ (the Messiah) this will turn out for my preservation (for the spiritual health and welfare of my own soul) *and* avail toward the saving work of the Gospel.... Christ (the Messiah) will be magnified *and* get glory *and* praise in this body of mine *and* be boldly exalted in my person, whether through (by) life or through (by) death" (Philippians 1:19,20, AMPC).

As our pastor says, "It is not about your condition, BUT your position"—position in Christ. So you can state your condition (circumstances) with confidence that your position (the truth of God's word you are standing on) will overcome!!

Why is it so important to know the difference between denial and faith? Well, I always believed this lie, that if you speak aloud of your circumstances then it is a sign of weakness in your faith. If everything is not perfect and going great in your life, you are not walking the true life of a faith believer. This is a lie straight from the father of all lies. I have discovered if you do not speak of what you are going through then the enemy can deceive you into thinking you are the only one going through these things. Then you tend to dwell on those lies.

Once it is spoken aloud to others, it is out there; and satan can no longer deceive you. You can still be tormented if you do not stand on God's promises. So seek His word/wisdom to stand against your circumstances. Pray the promise, not the problem.

Also, we need the encouragement of our brothers and sisters in Christ to get us through our difficult times in life. "For if they fall, the one will lift up his fellow. But woe to him who is alone when he falls and has not another to lift him up!" (Ecclesiastes 4:10.) Today I can rest in Him knowing that it is not about my condition, but my POSITION.

RESTING IN HIM

Brené Brown, in her book *The Gifts of Imperfection,* says, "Faith is a place of mystery, where we find the courage to believe in what we cannot see and the strength to let go of our fear of uncertainty." Well, there it is: uncertainty. For me that is the feeling of being out of control and vulnerable. What happens when I release control? I come to the end of myself and realize I in myself am powerless. That is a scary place to be for someone like me, a recovering control freak who needs to know the outcome.

When our family had to make a decision as to the next step of Dustan's medical treatment, we knew that we had to let go of our fear of the uncertainty. In the end, Dustan had the final say. We all had already prayed and were waiting for God's direction, but Dustan knew with all certainty that he was to take a step out of the boat. All along, God was in the boat with us. He was our anchor throughout all the storms. Now Dustan saw Him standing on the water and beckoning him forward.

Taking a step out of the boat is very risky. When Peter stepped out of the boat and walked on the water it might have seemed foolish to some. Peter wanted to be with Jesus, so he took a risk that God could do the impossible. If we have been called to take a risk we can be assured of several things: We will be challenged, have fear, doubt, and hesitation. Also, God's presence will be with us, and we will have the enabling of the Holy Spirit. I do not believe God will ever call us to nothing. He always has something better. "For my thoughts are not your thoughts, neither are your ways my ways, saith the Lord. For as the heavens are higher than the earth, so are my ways higher than your ways, and my thoughts than your thoughts" (Isaiah 55:8,9).

I often question whether Dustan knew something the rest of us did not know. Did Jesus give him a glimpse of heaven that he could not resist? Was he already so close to Jesus that he could only see through his spiritual eyes? I will never know the answers to these questions this side of heaven. One thing I do know is if Jesus gave me a glimpse of my forever home I am not sure I could ever look back. I believe I would run with such focus and excitement that nothing would distract me.

Taking a Step Out of the Boat

Now that I think about it, that was the look in my precious son's eyes on his last days. I never saw fear or anxiety, only hope and pure love in those big blue eyes. His words were few but encouraging. I think the most powerful was his silence and his constant smile. Peace at its finest.

All along our journey we knew God was sovereign over our lives. We knew He would never lead us down a path and then abandon us. So we stood on His promises and knew He would take care of Dustan. As we had to watch Dustan struggle with this horrible disease again we knew who would win the battle. God already had! As a mother it is very difficult to lay your child at the feet of Jesus and say, Thy will be done. That is where I was. I had to ask Jesus to give me peace with His will. I knew He loved Dustan and His will was for him to be completely healed. All good things come from God and only God.

Does this mean we had given up on this battle? NO! Every day we would get up with the anticipation that God would completely heal and restore Dustan's body. I believed God could heal him and I knew He would. I love the way Beth Moore says it, "God's will is always best even when we cannot imagine how. Surrendering to God's will does not mean you lose. Ultimately, it means you win." *(Paul: 90 Days on His Journey of Faith)*

*You see, I have not learned
to trust God in the easy ways of faith.
I have not learned to trust God by reading a book
or listening to a great sermon.
Nor have I learned to trust God by hearing
how my friend trusts God.
No, I am learning to trust God by stepping
out into an adventure of obedience, with no map,
and discovering for myself that He is trustworthy.*

—GLYNNIS WHITWER, NIV, REAL-LIFE DEVOTIONAL BIBLE FOR WOMEN

RESTING IN HIM

The plan of God for your life
is that you should be held captive
by His power, doing that which you
in the natural world would never do,
but that which you are forced to do
by the power of the Holy Ghost
moving through you.
—SMITH WIGGLESWORTH

When trying to accept an outcome much different from the one you prayed for, there's a fine line. You can try to place blame on something or someone; you can look for answers that would satisfy your broken heart; or, ultimately, I believe you just have to trust in the one who directs all things in your life when you surrender all to Him. I know we have a free will to make our own choices; but I also know that God helps us make those choices when we look to Him for the direction.

In *A Divine Invitation,* Steve McVey puts it like this:
>God 'ponders' all your goings (see Proverbs 5:21). The word denotes the idea of somebody walking alongside you with His face inches away from yours, carefully examining, scrutinizing, analyzing every move you make. Not only does God ponder your actions, but He even ponders your attitudes and the motivations that cause you to do the things you do (see Proverbs 21:2). Make no mistake about it, God has His eye on you and always has and always will.

This brings me so much comfort. It takes the stress off of me; if I do make a wrong decision or mistake, He is there. McVey also writes, "When the Apostle Peter found himself in water over his head, the Bible says that, 'beginning to sink, he cried out, "Lord, save me!" Immediately Jesus stretched out His hand and took hold of him' (Matthew 14:30,31, ESV). The Lord was teaching Peter the lesson

Taking a Step Out of the Boat

of faith and showing him the hopelessness of depending on self. God would never stand by and watch you drown in a sea of wrong decisions, despite the fact that at times you may feel otherwise. You can trust that God's strong arm is always reaching out on your behalf."

When cancer has engulfed your body and life, you come to place of complete powerlessness. The only control you have is how to react to the circumstances, and how you walk through the journey. This part of our journey, we were looking straight ahead at Jesus and walking on the water. We never once took our eyes off of Jesus.

CHAPTER 9

The Ultimate Sacrifice

*Now when David had served God's purpose
in his own generation, he fell asleep; he was buried
with his ancestors and his body decayed.*
(ACTS 13:36, NIV)

*Jesus said, 'This sickness will not end in death.
No, it is for God's glory so that God's Son
may be glorified through it.'*
(JOHN 11:4, NIV)

Dear Prayer Partners,
This is an e-mail I never wanted to send.

Dustan Noble Gammon is in the arms of his precious heavenly Father. He passed yesterday, Saturday, June 28, 2008, at 1:31 p.m. He has received his healing. He is now cancer free and pain free.

RESTING IN HIM

This past two months he did everything he wanted to do and enjoyed every minute. He was so strong and had the faith of a giant. His faith is what has taken him into his new life. The scripture we have truly clung to lately is, "I will not die, but live and declare the works of the Lord." I now realize this is a very powerful scripture. He did not die; he lives, and YES, he declared the works of the Lord. As does everyone he touched. So the works of the Lord will be declared every day.

>   F...*Forever*
>   A...*Always*
>   I.... *In*
>   T... *The*
>   H...*Heavens*

He held onto his Bible every day this past week. He knew he was close to going to his new home. He knew he was so close to his miracle. As we all know, he now has received it.

Now Dustan is resting in Him.

As I write the above words, it is just as hard seven years later as it was the day I penned them. There is a lighter side to my heart now. I have dug deep to find some truths that would make my heart smile instead of break. It has taken a very long painful journey, to say the least.

So many of the days leading up to Dustan's death have somewhat faded in my memories. I am very thankful that I have my journals that remind me of the conversations we had and the feelings that engulfed me at that time. One of my treasured findings right after his death was his devotional and Bible I found right next to his bed. The devotion was marked to a particular page that started out with, "PREPARING FOR LIFE...AND DEATH." The title brought me to my knees. Once I could compose myself enough to read the words on the page I found comfort in the words as I read slowly through each and every one. I will quote just this excerpt:

> *"Alive, I'm Christ's messenger; dead, I'm his bounty.*
> *Life versus even more life! I can't lose" (Philippians 1:21 MSG).*
>
> *God has given you the gift of life. How will you use that gift?*
> *Will you allow God's Son to reign over your heart?*
>
> *...Life is a glorious opportunity, but it is also shockingly brief.*
> *We must serve God each day as if it were our last day.*

On June 28, 2008, my life took an abrupt halt. Life as I knew it stopped. Everything started going in slow motion. I could hear everyone around me talking, but could not focus on anything. While sitting by Dustan's bedside all I wanted was everyone gone so I could hold Dustan and talk privately to him. But, everyone was there—because they too loved him.

When his last breath was taken my heart stopped. Everyone turned to someone for comfort. I stood in that room full of people alone; my precious son was not breathing any more, and everyone was crying and yelling—and they had no idea that I, his mother, had also stopped breathing. I was still standing, but I was not breathing. How could I breathe when my son was gone? Never to talk to me, hug me, laugh with me, argue with me; NOTHING. He was gone.

I couldn't believe it. *This didn't happen. Why am I in someone else's body going through this horrific event? Why?!*

After those moments I do not remember too much. I knew I had to leave the hospital and make all the plans to bury him. I didn't want to leave. I knew once I left, that was it. I would never again be able to look at that precious face—my son—so precious.

RESTING IN HIM

How can I leave him there and let others take his body and do God knows what to it? I can't leave him—even though he had already left me. I am leaving him at the hospital where, eighteen years before, I had left the hospital *with* him to start our new adventure together. Our first son, life so full of promise and hope—I did not know eighteen years later I would have to leave him at a hospital, to see him no more.

So much pain....

God's grace is amazing. I believe He does not allow a heart to take the full impact of a tragic event. I know that my heart would have exploded that day if it were not for the first stage of grief, numbing.

Do not get me wrong. I did feel like my heart was exploding. It was just like a bomb had gone off and I was hit with the flying shrapnel. Huge piece of metal sticking in my heart, small glass fragments piercing my eyes, and deafening ringing in my ears. I was walking through a war zone. I kept moving forward, but not really going anywhere.

Have you ever had one of those dreams that someone is chasing you and your feet are stuck and you cannot run? That is how I felt the weeks and months after Dustan passed. I had taken care of him, been by his side for thirty-one months. Now I had nothing.

I still had that motherly instinct that I should be running to something. Running toward our victory, Dustan's healing. My feet would not move. I think my heart knew more than my feet. My heart knew something was wrong, something was missing: my son. My feet still wanted to run. Now that I look back maybe I was trying to outrun the pain. Nope, that was impossible. Wherever I went the pain went with me.

Mornings were excruciating for me. Each day as soon as my eyes opened reality would slap me in the face. MY BABY IS GONE! Then it was if someone had cut out my heart and left me to bleed to death. Every single day I would have the same conversation with myself:

The Ultimate Sacrifice

Now April, you know joy comes in the morning.

It is morning. There's no joy. Dustan is not here.

I would hear that still, small voice softly whisper, "God is love and I know He loves me. He only wants good for me. If He allowed Dustan to go home then He knows things I do not know. He knows best; He has my best interest at heart." I would drag myself out of the bed at that instant, before I could talk myself out of getting up. You see, I knew if there was ever a day I did not choose to get out of that bed, that would be the day I would never get up again.

I remember reading a comment that Beth Moore had written when she asked her mother-in-law how she survived the death of her son. Her mother-in-law simply said, "I just kept breathing and getting up." I could so relate to this comment. I just had to keep breathing and getting up. And that is exactly what I did day after day.

Days turned into weeks and then months. My pain surrounded me; it engulfed me—at times, it would completely take me out.

I remember the silence being overwhelming. Dylan was back in school, Kenny was back to work, I was all alone. I remember wishing I could get back on that Ugly Monster roller-coaster ride again. Then we would all be together as we were supposed to be.

I knew the truth was that I could not wish that on Dustan again. It was selfish of me to want to go back. I did not like that violent ride; and yet this one was so much worse. With the roller-coaster ride, I felt we were being carried and led on our path. In the House of Mirrors, we were having to walk and find own way.

The House of Mirrors can be a fun and exciting adventure if you know the truth of who you are and whose you are. It does not matter what you see in the mirrors because you know it's just an illusion. Just like at the end of the movie *Grease*, when Danny and Sandy enter the House of Mirrors and are having fun going up and down on the moving floor. They are laughing and enjoying the ride. Why?!

They have discovered they belong together and they are going to adapt to make it work. Both change the way they dress, each tries to conform to the other. When Danny sees Sandy, he realizes and at the same moment so does she, they are willing to make changes. Now in all reality, I think Danny just thought Sandy was hot, but you get the gist of it. As the song at the end says, "We Go Together."

We knew that we belonged together; Dustan, Dylan, Kenny, and I. We knew we belonged to Christ. "If we live, we live for the Lord; and if we die, we die for the Lord. Therefore, whether we live or die, we belong to the Lord" (Romans 14:8, HCSB). Romans 12:5, "So it is with Christ's body. We are many parts of one body, and we all belong to each other" (NLT).

Whether together here on earth, or in heaven—we knew we'd always be together, forever. What we did not know is how we were going to walk that truth out. In I Corinthians 13:12, "For now we see only a reflection as in a mirror; then we shall see face to face. Now I know in part; then I shall know fully, even as I am fully known." I really love how The Message states it, "We don't yet see things clearly. We're squinting in a fog, peering through a mist. But it won't be long before the weather clears and the sun shines bright! We'll see it all then, see it all as clearly as God sees us, knowing him directly just as he knows us!"

Before we could get to the place of knowing who we really were and what we really believed about God and our faith, we had to go through the room of the distorted mirrors. Our foundation as we knew it had cracked.

I am not saying that what we believed before Dustan's passing was not right. We just needed to revisit our own belief system.

The Ultimate Sacrifice

God will use all circumstances in your life for you to see Him more clearly. Our view of God and His love had become clouded. Don't get me wrong, we did not turn our backs on God at any time during our grief. Oh, on the contrary; without Him we could not have survived this journey. Even on the days we thought we could not hear Him, He was there.

So many days I would look in my physical mirror and think, Who am I? What do I believe? Why is this happening to me? Just like those mirrors at the carnival, each mirror would show me something different. I just had to figure out which mirror was showing me the truth. Little did I know that was going to be a very long, lonely, painful, soul-searching journey.

I would like to say I did not have a choice, but I did. I could have chosen to stay there and drown in my grief, I could have pushed it all down and pretended everything was okay, I even could have found alternatives to mask my pain. Honestly, all of these would have been so much easier than looking in the mirror and seeing what was looking back at me.

The ultimate sacrifice is the Father giving His Son to the cross. Oh, how He must love us. This momma could not have given up her son to die for those who loved him; or, even worse, those who did not. Even if I could see what our Father sees I am not sure my choice would be any different. The agony of letting go and watching Dustan take his last breath is in no way a comparison to Mary watching Jesus hang on that cross and die for others. Although, I am sure our mothers' hearts broke just the same. Jesus had promised He was coming back in three days, and Mary believed Him. Before Jesus took His last breath one of His final cries was, "It is finished." What was finished? It was not only Christ's earthly life, not only His suffering and dying, not only the payment for sin and the *redemption* of the world—but the very reason and purpose He came to earth was finished. His final act of obedience was complete. The scriptures had been fulfilled. Jesus knew He was going home.

RESTING IN HIM

I know I cannot compare my son to Jesus, but to me he was everything. When he was lying in that hospital bed and I was watching his chest rise up and down I knew he was still with me, physically anyway. The moment he gasped and let out that last breath, I knew "it was finished." He was at home in the arms of Jesus. He had fulfilled his purpose. No more suffering, no more pain. Mine, on the other hand, was just beginning. As hard as it was to watch him disappear into a place I could not even fathom, I knew he was at peace. Finally.

Acts 14:36,37, "For when David had served God's purpose in his own generation, he fell asleep; he was buried with his fathers and his body decayed. But the one whom God raised from the dead did not see decay" (NIV). I do believe Dustan served his purpose in his eighteen years on earth, and he accomplished more than most his age. I do not dwell on the fact that his body may decay. I know he is not there. He is in heaven being busy about our Father's work. One day soon we will all be together forever.

When people speak of a loved one passing they use the word loss. I do not use that word when I speak of Dustan because I did not lose him. I know where he is. But I have lost his physical "earth suit," which hurts me deeply. His presence will always be with me, but his earth suit has been placed away for safekeeping.

I do not visit his grave often. I know wherever I am, he is always with me. When I walk through our house I see him everywhere. When I look at Kenny there is always a reflection of who Dustan was. When I hear Dylan laugh I can still hear Dustan's sweet giggle. When other people speak of him it's as if I can see him in their stories. So I love to talk about him; I feel it keeps him alive in our home.

I remember one day when it hit me really hard that our language involving Dustan was changing. It was around about the eight-month mark of his passing. Just in general conversation I used the words "Dustan used to...." I stopped dead in my tracks and my heart just sank. Up until that point I could still say he *just said*, he *just did*, he *just told me*. It was at that moment I realized I would never again say "just."

The Ultimate Sacrifice

Oxford defines *just* as "very recently; in the immediate past." The synonyms are: "a moment ago, a second ago, a short time ago, and not long ago."

"I just saw him." For me, that immediate past was going away. It was then I realized there would never be a recent event with him ever again. Still peering through the fog of numbness, I was starting to feel the pin pricks of my reality.

As reality set in, these are the words I penned:

I just do not know what to say. How do I feel? Are there words? I cannot find any. Words just seem to escape me right now. Each day gets harder and harder. Each day is like another piece of me being peeled away, those pieces that have been protecting my heart, my so-called strong heart. Now, each day another piece of my heart is peeled off; and I feel the rawness of what is left. The rawness of grief. The roughness, yet tender part of my heart. The part that is left to feel what is missing. The part that beats with sorrow each second of the day. The part that you're afraid might not beat again because the pain is so intense.

Does anyone understand? I am afraid they do not. They think they can, and they try, but it's just impossible. Their hearts hurt with grief over losing someone they knew. My heart hurts with grief over losing my life, a part of me. That part of my life that I delighted in every second of the day. The son I carried for nine months close to my heart; he knew my heartbeat well. The son whose every need I cared for. The son that was/is an extension of who I am, the son who, when I looked at him, my heart would jump with joy. The son I now remember but cannot look at, and my heart jumps with sorrow.

Is jump even the right word? I don't think so. My heart does not jump any more, it just lies dormant. The stillness of grief/sorrow with each beat I feel is the beat of loss. The loss of not only my precious, sweet son, but the loss of a part of myself. The only part of me of which I can say, This is good—he is good—I did something right.

RESTING IN HIM

For me, I knew I had to journal. I needed a place to put down my raw emotion. Even though I say words escaped me, words came flowing on my pages. Every day I would write what my mouth could not say and others dare not hear. It was being the real me. Journaling gave me a place to be who I really was.

The sad thing is, I had to figure out: who was I? This is where my daily visit of the mirrors began. Those images in the mirrors surrounded me. It was like a horror show. If I did not like what I saw in one mirror I would run away as fast as I could, only to find that I ran right into the middle of another. These mirrors haunted me day and night. Remember, in the House of Mirrors the images are distorted. One could make you look fat, skinny, tall, short, another could enlarge your head, or give you a monster figure. My mirrors showed me fear, lies, deception, perfectionism, graven images, and the worst of all, the person I had created for others to see.

My companions had become Sorrow and Suffering, as depicted in *Hinds' Feet on High Places*; the protagonist, named Much-Afraid, desires to escape her Fearing relatives. She goes with the Shepherd to the High Places where "perfect love casteth out fear." Her Shepherd gives her two companions, Sorrow and Suffering, to take along with her on the journey. I could not have guessed how God would use this allegory to transform me into the little handmaiden "Acceptance with Joy," as Much-afraid was transformed. The author's hope was "for the reader to grow in accepting and triumphing over evil, becoming acquainted with grief and pain, and, ultimately, finding them transformed into something incomparably precious; learning through constant glad surrender to know the Lord of Love Himself in a new way and to experience unbroken union with Him." That is exactly what happened to me.

We did not realize it at the time, but our foundation began to shake the day Dustan was diagnosed. We did not recognize the signs because we were dumped on the Ugly Monster roller-coaster. We did not see the cracks, or the potholes starting to form, and the major sinkhole in the center. As we did our twists, turns, and twirls on the Ugly Monster, everything else was out of our sight.

The Ultimate Sacrifice

It was when we were forced to exit and shoved into the House of Mirrors that we began to notice the shaking of what was beneath us. It was then we had to make a decision, and it had to be made pretty quickly. Were we going to try to mend our foundation or were we going to let everything break away and stand on what little we knew to be true. As we huddled together, we three, we knew we could stand on God's love. So our small little circle of foundation had to be enough until we could start building the rest.

There were a lot of things we had to give up the day we said goodbye to Dustan's body. We all had to give up a piece of our hearts; but the common denominator for each of us was that voice of reason and encouragement that had kept our family of four grounded. Dustan had been the level-headed one, always calm, and looking at the bright side of every situation. He was a lot like his dad in that way.

Now our four-legged table was unbalanced. It was time for a family shift. Our table was under construction and I was not sure how it was going to turn out. I personally always like the look of a four-legged table better than the three-legged kind. It just seemed to me that it was sturdier, and could withstand more weight or impact. Not really having a choice, we were going to rebuild our table. We were not going to let what had happened to our family define us. We were going to take what was left, our broken and shattered three-legged table, and make it better than ever.

Giving back is easy when you have all you need and want. It takes nothing. It takes everything to give back when you have lost the world.

That one something or someone that means everything to you, that is your world. When we are at our weakest is when God does the mightiest. "And he said unto me, 'My grace is sufficient for thee: for my strength is made perfect in weakness.' Most gladly therefore will I rather glory in my infirmities, that the power of Christ may rest upon me" (II Corinthians 12:9).

RESTING IN HIM

I did not know the full impact of this scripture until, at my weakest place, I found His grace. His grace is what covered me when our new construction began. It was His grace that helped us build our beautiful new table.

The ultimate sacrifice for mankind was God giving His Son so that we all should have life and have it everlasting. John 3:16 tells us of the love God has for us and the extent of that love—so great that He sacrificed His only Son on our behalf. *John 3:16* teaches us that anyone who believes in Jesus Christ, God's Son, will be saved. *John 3:16* gives us the glorious hope of eternal life in heaven through the love of God and death of Jesus Christ.

Our family's ultimate sacrifice was Dustan's earthly life for our newfound spiritual life. When everything else was stripped away all that was left was God's love. Our eyes were opened to the true unconditional love of our Father. Dustan's death propelled us into a real relationship with our Father.

It was no longer about religion, it was now all about His love. We had found our hope in Christ.

The Ultimate Sacrifice

Family beach vacation, Grayton Beach, Fla., summer 2006

Our new normal, March 2013

CHAPTER 10

The Healing Process

He heals the brokenhearted and binds up their wounds.
(PSALM 147:3, NIV)

His family all tried to comfort him, but he refused to be comforted. 'I will go to my grave mourning for my son,' he would say, and then he would weep.
(GENESIS 37:35, NLT)

Good Evening My Friends,

It has been a while since I wrote. I wish I could say everything has been good but I cannot. It is still so hard and every day seems to get harder. It has been seven months, ten days, and six hours. Oh, just the pain to write that.

Please keep us in your prayers. As if losing your son weren't enough to deal with we still have to deal with the everyday things of life. Whew!

The God I serve is able.

RESTING IN HIM

My relationship with my heavenly Father is more than I ever thought it could be. Who else can listen to my rambling thoughts and still love me unconditionally? Okay, besides my sweet husband. When I am screaming at the top of my lungs that I cannot do it any more, I hear Him whisper: No, but I can. *When I am jumping up and down saying WHY?!, He whispers,* Because I love you. *When I continue to argue with Him, He whispers,* I will weep with you.

I am so glad I can crawl through this journey with Him. For without Him, I am nothing and could do nothing. I give Him all the praise and all the glory.

I took Dustan for granted. Perhaps we all take each other too much for granted. The routines of life distract us; our own anxieties and sorrows make us unmindful. The beauties of the familiar go unremarked. We do not treasure each other enough.

He was a gift to us for eighteen years. When the gift was gone, I realized how great it was. Then I could not tell him. An outpouring of letters arrived, many expressing how wonderful he was. They all made me weep again, each word another stab of loss. How can I be thankful, in his absence, for what he was? I find I am. But the pain of the no more *outweighs the gratitude of the* once was. *Will it always be so?*

I didn't know how much I loved him until he was gone.

Dylan wrote this and I could see my sweet Dustan saying these words:

Dad, have no worries when you think of me;
I'm living the stories told by the King of kings.
I'm completely healed and without tears.
Let your heart be still for the remaining years.
I know some days can be rough;
Just renew your mind when things get tough.
Think of all the good times that we had.

The Healing Process

I love you so much—
You were an incredible dad.
You loved me well, and continue to.
I'll be here waiting as He watches over you.

Brother, there were times when I prayed for you
When you thought my mind couldn't stay with you.
I've held our conversations close to my heart
As I am there within yours, never far apart.
Admitting your weakness is a sign of strength.
Love your dearest ones until your last blink.
Be my eyes and ears for Father and Mother.
I love you so much—
You were an incredible brother.
You loved me well, and continue to.
I'll be here waiting as He watches over you.

Mom, I know you think of me every day,
Trying to think of my thoughts and the words I would say:
My laugh, my voice, my touch may seem to fade,
But the spirit of me will always remain.
I know you miss me and cry sometimes,
But I'm resting in Him; please keep that in mind.
I love you so much—
You were an incredible mom.
You loved me well, and continue to.
I'll be here waiting as He watches over you.

Death leaves a heartache no one can heal, love leaves a memory no one can steal.

Resting in Him, April

RESTING IN HIM

Reading words about loss, pain, emptiness, sadness, and the grieving process brought me such comfort. I know that sounds ironic. I just needed to know that I was not the only one having these feelings and thinking these thoughts. When you try to make sense of what your family has just gone through, the thoughts in your head can get all mixed up. I remember a conversation between Kenny and me within the first couple of months after Dustan's passing. We were sitting together not saying anything, and yet we both understood what each was thinking. About the same moment we looked at each and said, "Are we crazy?"

I just wished these thoughts would slow down. We knew we needed counsel. We needed someone who understood the grief process. If we did not get a handle on what was happening we were going to drown in our sorrow. As Christians we knew the first place to go was to His word. One of His promises is that He will never leave you nor forsake you. Our heads knew, but our hearts were so broken we just could not feel that truth. We started crying out to God in our deepest sorrow and pain to send someone in our direction who could help us make sense of this all. And He was faithful. He led us to a new community of people that would change our lives. This community surrounded us, prayed for us, met us in our darkest places, and most of all held us up when we were slumped over in agony.

In Psalm 18:4–6 (NET), "The waves of death engulfed me, the currents of chaos overwhelmed me. The ropes of Sheol tightened around me, the snares of death trapped me. In my distress I called to the Lord; I cried out to my God. From his heavenly temple he heard my voice; he listened to my cry for help" (New English Translation). The NLT says it this way, "The ropes of death entangled me; floods of destruction swept over me. The grave wrapped its ropes around me; death laid a trap in my path. But in my distress I cried out to the Lord; yes, I prayed to my God for help. He heard me from his sanctuary; my cry to him reached his ears."

We had a rope of despair around our necks. Every day it was getting tighter and tighter. We were starting to lose our breath. We were gasping for air with no help in

The Healing Process

sight. Sadly, there were people around us pushing us farther and farther under. We needed a respite. In God's faithfulness he sent us people who would be an intricate part of our healing process. He brought people from our past, people from our present, and others who would be essential to our future.

I am sure you have heard the grief process described as walking through waves. As a little girl I remember going to the beach with my family. One of my treasured memories is when my dad would wade out in the ocean while pulling me on a float with a little window in the center. I did not like to wade very far out. Even as a small child I did not like the unknowns. Things would brush up against my legs or touch my toes; I would shrink with terror. So my dad would come to my rescue and pull me out into the deep on the safety of my little pink float. I would giggle as I looked through the window at the things underwater.

I was safe. It was so much fun when the waves would come quickly and propel me toward the beach. I would laugh and throw my head back. I enjoyed it so when I knew Dad had hold of the rope attached to my little float.

Until one time, this huge wave came crashing toward us and Dad lost hold of the rope. I wasn't scared, because I could still see my dad beside me. I knew as long as he was there everything was okay. He swam quickly to grab the rope; but it slipped away. Again he reached it; but it would slip through his fingers every time. I still was not worried. I knew he would save me. Then the biggest of the waves came, and I was tipped over. That's when the terror of the deep hit me. Now, I knew I could swim. Getting to the shore was not a problem. I had to swim through all the unknowns under the water that would brush up against me or try to take me down; that was my biggest fear. So I just started swinging my little arms and legs as fast as they would tread. I felt things touch me, and so I tried to move faster—to no avail. I looked for my dad, could not find him anywhere. My safety was gone! Even though my dad had told me on many occasions what to do if I fell off my float, my mind would not think that fast. Eventually, instinct kicked in and I dog-paddled until I could reach the sandy floor. At that very moment I felt Dad's arms around me. He found me and rescued me. When he asked me if I was okay, my lips could not speak fast enough of the scary ordeal: that the waves kept overwhelming me, I could not find my footing, and lastly, "Where were you, Dad? I needed you."

My dad smiled and said, "I was right here honey, I never left you."

He said, "Even though I did not have hold of the rope I never lost sight of you. I knew I could get to you when you needed me." And that he did!

Our journey of grief was like that. Our heavenly Father was always there. In those moments I could not see Him, He never took His eyes off us. Those overwhelming times when grief nearly drowned me, His gaze was upon me. Psalm 33:18–22 (NIV),

> But the eyes of the Lord are on those who fear him, on those whose hope is in his unfailing love, to deliver them from death and keep them alive in famine. We wait in hope for the Lord; he is our help and our shield. In him our hearts rejoice, for we trust in his holy name. May your unfailing love be with us, Lord, even as we put our hope in you.

What can be most overwhelming about grief is the loneliness. In the first few months there are lots of people around, cards, e-mails, phone calls, and meals. Then like a slow rain shower, everyone and everything fades away in the gloom of the storm.

There are those well meaning people who tell you what you need to do and how to do it so you can snap back to your old selves again. Then there are those who seem to have just disappeared from your lives. Others try to say something to comfort you because they in themselves feel so uncomfortable with the situation. Honestly, I could write another book on what to say, what not to say, and how to be there for someone who is grieving. That's a whole separate subject.

I did learn in the process of our own grieving that grace is an amazing thing: not only to receive grace from others, but also how to extend that grace when faced

The Healing Process

with your deepest hurts and sorrows. I know people mean well, and it has taken me a long time to be okay with that. I've learned that some people are good at just sitting with you in your grief and others run as fast as they can. I am still okay with that. The bottom line is, if they love you and understand the grace process they will be there for you eventually, exactly in the right season of your life.

Let's get back to the waves of grief. Grief is defined as "intense sorrow, especially caused by someone's death." Ocean waves can be defined as a "disturbance on the surface of a body of water, in the form of a moving ridge or swell."

"When studying waves, it is important to note that while it appears the water is moving forward, only a small amount of water is actually moving. Instead, it is the wave's energy that is moving and since water is a flexible medium for energy transfer, it looks like the water itself is moving" (Amanda Briney, "Ocean Waves.")

Interesting, don't you think? In the grieving process doesn't it seem at times you are moving forward, when in reality, it is only a small part of you that is moving? Just like the water, you look to be moving forward as a whole; and yet so many pieces of you are still stuck, not moving at all. Let's face it, to be moving forward at all is a huge accomplishment.

For our family, we felt like someone stuck all of us on a speedboat, took us as far as we could go into the center of the ocean, and threw us overboard. I was praying for my little pink float again and that my dad was there to rescue me. We were bobbing up and down, waves overtaking us. Just as my dad had rescued me right at the moment I needed him, I knew that my heavenly Father would rescue us. He seemed to be far off in the distance. My little pink float had disappeared. I did not see any safety devices to grab hold of. We were way out in the deep trying to keep our heads above the water.

At times we would fight against the current, we would try to swim as fast as we could, and we would dog-paddle until our bodies were exhausted. There were even those times we would lie back in the waters and just float. That's when we were

RESTING IN HIM

truly resting in Him, when we could forget everything around us and just relax and float with the waves of the water, the waves of our grief. Somewhere in that place where fiction collides with reality, we realized we have to keep fighting, keep moving to get to the shore, the shore of our new normal.

"In the open ocean, the friction moving the waves generates energy within the water. This energy is then passed between water molecules in ripples called waves of transition. When the water molecules receive the energy, they move forward slightly and form a circular pattern. As the water's energy moves forward toward the shore and the depth decreases, the diameter of these circular patterns also decreases" (Briney). As with grief, the friction is the resistance of dealing with the pain, which can cause a negative energy in your life. The negative energy keeps you bobbing up and down. You don't want to face the intense feelings of your loss so you keep smiling and saying everything is okay even when you are dying on the inside.

The waves of transition take on a life all to themselves. Some people cling to what used to be before a death. Our family knew we needed something new and different. We had ridden the Ugly Monster for almost three years and it was time to make a change. We knew we could not live in our son's death. We were choosing to live in his life.

We could not bob up and down in the deep waters any more. We needed to swim. We could see the shore off in the distance and we were going to do whatever it took to make it to land even if that meant losing sight of the shore. There's a great quote by Andre Gide, "Man cannot discover new oceans unless he has the courage to lose sight of the shore." There was a new ocean for us; we just had to take our eyes off of ourselves and put them onto Jesus.

Please don't be mistaken and think we decided one day that we were going to move forward and everything was going to work out great! Once we made the decision not to live in the tragedy of Dustan's death, but to celebrate him and live in the beauty of his life—the full eighteen years—there were many transitions that had to take place for us to move forward in a healthy grieving process.

Though uncertain how to accomplish it, we just knew we would not let his death be in vain.

"Because waves move in groups, they continue arriving behind the first and all of the waves are forced closer together since they are now moving slower. They then grow in height and steepness. When the waves become too high relative to the water's depth, the wave's stability is undermined and the entire wave topples onto the beach forming a breaker" (Briney).

In our healing process we began to make changes that would help us to grieve at a slower pace. We did not just adopt the mentality to suck it up and move forward without feeling our pain. We found out the hard way that for us to live in Dustan's life and not death, we needed to heal from all of our broken places. This was not and *still* is not an easy task. It's examining everything in your life that led up to the death and everything in your life that will help you move forward. We found out pretty quickly that we had a lot of broken places that needed Jesus to come into and heal.

It's amazing how a horrific loss will cause such a ripple effect with all your other losses. Just as waves move in groups, so are the scars of your losses. As you start to examine and try to heal from one loss, then another one will come right behind, and then another, until they are forced together. Then they gain intensity and depth. When they become too much to deal with, then your stability is undermined and the entire process of your healing topples and forms a breaker, the breaking point.

This breaking point brought forth all our festering wounds. Psalm 38:5–11 (NIV),

My wounds fester and are loathsome because of my sinful folly.
I am bowed down and brought very low; all day long I go about mourning.
My back is filled with searing pain; there is no health in my body.
I am feeble and utterly crushed; I groan in anguish of heart.

RESTING IN HIM

All my longings lie open before you, Lord; my sighing is not hidden from you. My heart pounds, my strength fails me; even the light has gone from my eyes. My friends and companions avoid me because of my wounds; my neighbors stay far away.

A decision to be made: Were we going to nurse our wounds? All our wounded places came floating to the top as we were walking through our healing. We were reacting to other wounds that had not completely healed. It was like picking a scab over and over. We knew that wounded people hurt people. We had experienced this in so many ways. We were wounded deeply and we were trying to live life, make decisions and find healing; and we were not doing it perfectly. It was time to look at everything in our lives that was keeping us from being healthy and whole. Just like weeds in a garden. If you do not pull them up immediately they will become rooted and spread quickly.

Isaiah 1:6 (NIV), "From the sole of your foot to the top of your head there is no soundness— only wounds and welts and open sores, not cleansed or bandaged or soothed with olive oil." We did not want to live our lives as wounded, hurt people. We wanted others to see Jesus in us. The only way for that to happen is for us to open ourselves up and let Jesus begin the healing. To pull all the scabs and let His word and His love be the salve for our wounds.

The pain of our recovery was much harder than the injury. The degree to which we were willing to embrace the pain is the degree to which we would find our full recovery. We were willing to break up all the scar tissue.

Yes, we were broken, crushed, and oozing with deep emotion. Everything and anything would set us off. We were walking a tight rope and any little movement or sound would cause us to shake. Possibly even fall.

Then one day, it happened. Sights and sounds kept coming at us and we could not keep it together any more. As we were beginning to fall we tried to grasp the rope, but our hands slipped right by it. Now we were in free fall not knowing if there was a net below. We had nothing left to hang onto so we all grabbed each other as we began to descend.

I love the quote by Yo-Yo Ma, "Things can fall apart, or threaten to, for many reasons, and then there's got to be a leap of faith. Ultimately, when you're at the edge, you have to go forward or backward; if you go forward, you have to jump together." We jumped and we jumped big.

I want to be truthful and say, I was the one who hit my grief head-on first. Thankfully, God had a plan even in my disarray of grief. He could see what good was going to come from this deep, dark chaos. I believe I already shared with you that I was a perfectionist, control freak, and a very black-or-white person. So God knew it was going to take some real shaking and some deep cleaning to make me more like him. It was going to take my looking at the deepest part of my soul to see which mirror was telling me the truth. The House of Mirrors was getting ready to be my resting place for a while.

July 2010

Oh Lord—Why do my thoughts seem to be so overwhelming? Why does my mind go in so many directions? Why can I not focus on what is in front of me? I know the enemy would love for me to stay bogged down; BUT I know you came to give me life and freedom. Open my eyes to see you, Lord. Open my heart to receive your healing. I know I have so many issues; BUT I also know you can walk through them with me. I choose to trust you and only YOU! I pray for restoration of ALL we have lost. All the relationships that have been destroyed, all emotions that seem to be buried; you can revive and bring to life all that has died. Let me not fear all that you have for me. You are good and all that you have for me is good.

My heart cries out to you, O Lord!
You are my friend and my salvation,
To whom I give everything.

RESTING IN HIM

Psalm 27:1 (NIV),
The Lord is my light and my salvation—whom shall I fear?
The Lord is the stronghold of my life—of whom shall I be afraid?

Beth Moore did a study on the healing of your wounds. Several things stuck with me as I was journeying through my own healing process. In one of her broadcasts, I remember hearing her say, "A broken heart heals when we allow the healing to go as deep as the wound went." Wow! May not be rocket science, but for me it was life changing. I was not going to get over my son's passing in a few months or even years. He was a part of my life every day for eighteen years. Why would I think I would be healed in a few short years?

It was if God whispered to me and said, *It is okay to hurt, to be angry, to be sad; it is okay to have all the emotions. I am here and we will walk this out together, however long it takes.*

In the beginning of my grief journey I remember so many people would tell me I must accept this loss and move on. To me this was nothing more than denial of how important my son was to me. I could not and would not deny my pain. I decided to surround myself with people who loved me and encouraged me to walk through this pain: those who would on many occasions grab my hand and walk the lonely distant walk of grief with me.

I have to be honest, most of the time I had to walk this path with only my heavenly Father as my companion. The pain was too deep for anyone to understand or even see. He would on many of those walks squeeze my hand so I knew He was there, and then other times He held it loosely so I would feel my own freedom to walk. My path, as so many others' who have endured the same pain, got very, very dark. It was a tortuous path to travel. Even to this day I can gaze in the eyes of Dustan in a photo and my heart aches with such intensity that I can barely breathe.

The Healing Process

I could deny that pain and walk right by those photos and not even give it a second thought. Oh! I would much rather look into the eyes of my son and remember the love and bond we had as mother and son. As much as it hurts it is far superior to trying to escape or deny that pain. Psalm 34:8 (ESV), *Taste and see that the Lord is good; blessed is the man who takes refuge in him.* And Ecclesiastes 3:11 (ESV), *He has made everything beautiful in its time.* He will take all my pain and make it beautiful in his timing.

Largely alone with these emotions, I needed to read about loss and others' heartache. One book was *Lament for a Son* by Nicholas Wolterstorff. Talk about a book with raw emotion. This one was it. I found it sadly refreshing. I was reading my own emotions in black and white, on paper. It was if this man knew and felt my every emotion.

His son had died in a cliff climbing accident. Even with our differences, the pain resonated with me just the same. One term he used was his "mourning bench." That was such a powerful visual with me. When you think of a bench you think of sitting. I needed people to sit with me. Not to say a word, not to fix the situation, not to make me feel better. I just needed someone there. I love the way he puts it his book.

> If you think your task as comforter is to tell me that really, all things considered, it's not so bad, you do not sit with me in my grief but place yourself off in the distance away from me. Over there, you are of no help. What I need to hear from you is that you recognize how painful it is. I need to hear from you that you are with me in my desperation. To comfort me, you have to come close. Come sit beside me on my mourning bench.

He talks about how hard it was for others to comfort him, because many were uncomfortable with their own feelings. They stumbled on their words, or said nothing at all. But, "Your tears are salve on our wound," he says; "your silence is salt."

RESTING IN HIM

Most importantly, he says, after more time had passed, when people would ask how he was doing, the true comforters were those who would stop him and ask, *"No, I mean really,"* if he'd given a quick "Okay" or "Fine."

Oh my! I so could have penned these words myself. My mourning bench was not comfortable. It was made with hard, skinny planks that would make my guest wiggle in the place next to me. It was hard to sit on and it was not for the faint of heart. If you were uncomfortable with silence then you did not stay long; if you could not handle the emotions that would seep from my broken heart you would just disappear without a trace. But for those who would sit with me day after day, you were the witness of a beautiful transformation. "No one else can know your sadness, and strangers cannot share your joy" (Proverbs 14:10, NCV).

My mourning bench became a revolving swing. So many would hang on and ride it out with me, and others would come and go. The beauty of the revolving swing was God placed exactly who I needed there to sit with me at exactly the right time. I love how God brings people in your life for a reason, a season, or a lifetime. I've learned to embrace all three. The one for a reason is to meet a need, maybe for guidance or support; the one for a season—because it's your turn to share, grow, or learn; and the one for a lifetime is to teach you those lessons that will help throughout your life.

> *The friend who can be silent with us*
> *in a moment of despair or confusion,*
> *who can stay with us in an hour of*
> *grief and bereavement,*
> *who can tolerate not knowing,*
> *not curing, not healing...,*
> *that is a friend who cares.*
> —HENRI NOUWEN

The Healing Process

Today my bench is not made out of hard planks. It's made out of beautiful refurbished crafted pieces that have become a resting place for others to look upon in their own time of grief. I will invite you to sit with me while I share of how our gracious heavenly Father remade it piece by piece. Anything that is worth looking upon is worth the hard work and time it takes to make it beautiful. It has taken a very long time for God to make me an open book so that others whose bench is just now being built will have hope that their bench can be as beautiful as mine.

CHAPTER 11

Treasures I Found In the Dark

*I will give you hidden treasures,
riches stored in secret places,
so that you may know that I am the Lord,
the God of Israel, who summons you by name.
(ISAIAH 45:3, NIV)*

Hello Everyone,

The last few days I have been thinking a lot about each of you. How much your prayers, support, and love have gotten us through a very difficult time. There is nothing like the support of family and friends. Now as we continue to journey through our life we still need each of you.

RESTING IN HIM

This past week another family we know has been struck by leukemia, and another lost their battle. Why is it we lose one, and another seems to take his place in the battle? Why? I have learned there are no answers to WHY, not yet. I have also learned to not ask why. I just trust that my heavenly Father knows what is best for each of us. Yes, you could ask why, if He knows what is best for us, then why do bad things happen to good people. I've learned not to play the WHY game. It undermines trust. We all have questions we would like the answers to, but if we knew the answers would there not be still another WHY?

You see, we live in a world where we want everything just like we want it. We have our dreams, our hopes, and our desires. The real question is, Are these dreams, hopes, and desires ours or God's? I envisioned my family of four being together forever—maybe adding more when the boys got married and had children. That was my dream, my hope, and my desire. Yet, this did not seem to be our path. I think, WHY would God not want our family together? WHY? Would this not be His plan? God's ultimate plan is for family to be together forever. Sometimes life happens and our circumstances turn out unlike our dreams we have envisioned. He sees the bigger picture. Even though my heart breaks I know this is our path now. Wherever you land, God has a plan. Who am I to question His plan? As long as I know I am walking in fellowship with Him and following where He leads then the WHYs are irrelevant.

Perfect peace is what we seek. To have perfect peace you cannot ask WHY. The WHYs will lead you to a road you do not want to travel, a road that never seems to end but continues in circles. We must step out. Stop asking why. Just continue holding our Father's hand and walk the road He leads. He will never lead us astray. In spite of my questions and pain, I am not willing to exchange my limited knowledge for God's sovereignty. Only God knows the purpose that will come from our loss and our pain. I trust Him!

The scripture Jeremiah 29:11 says, "For I know the plans I have for you," declares the Lord, "plans to prosper you and not to harm you, plans to give you hope and a future." He knows the plan for our lives and it is only for good. Our hope and future is in Him, whether on earth or in heaven. If I believe His word I must believe all of it. This scripture should help us not ask the whys. Just to say, Yes, Lord, and amen.

Please be in prayer for the two families I have mentioned above. God is still a good God. He still performs miracles. We must trust His plan for our lives.

Chris Tomlin's song "I Will Rise" expresses my heart's cry. AND I WILL RISE.... This is what I hear my precious Dustan singing: Mom, I will rise!!! There will be no more tears nor pain. I will rise on that glorious day.

If we are His children we will all RISE!!!

Dustan had the faith of a giant, and never ever did he ask why. He just trusted.

Resting in Him, knowing my Dustan will RISE, April

It's amazing that I wrote the above update just four months after Dustan passed. I think I was just getting myself ready to travel that WHY road. It was not too long after that I penned these words:

> *Oh Lord, the whys are so hard.*
> *Why so soon?*
> *Why now?*
> *Why when he had so much to give?*
> *Why when he believed so hard?*
> *Why when he trusted you so much?*
> *Why him?*
> *Why when his earthly testimony was so big?*
> *Why us?*

RESTING IN HIM

Why when our faith was so strong?
Why when he had already been through so much?
Why when he was doing so good?
Why cancer?
Why so much pain?
Why death?
WHY, WHY, WHY???????

I remember on so many occasions crying out to God, *WHY? Why my son?* Then one day in the silence before my next wail, I heard Him speak to my heart: "April, what if I gave you the answers to all your whys? Would it be enough? Would it satisfy your broken heart?"

At first my answer was, *Yes, it would help.* Then, as I sat with the whys churning through my mind, I knew there was no answer that would have been good enough for me. My son was gone. It did not matter why. I wanted him here with me.

I do question why. I may never know the answer here on earth. But I do know that the Lord is my answer. I trust Him with all that is inside me. What else or who else is there but Him? I thank him for slowly opening my eyes to see the blessing of this pain and sorrow.

It is hard to believe that there are blessings from Dustan's passing. There are spiritual blessings. I see God more clearly than I ever have. I see my life and people so differently. If Kenny, Dylan, and I can change from this then we can trust the Lord. I am learning what love really is and is not. I still ponder the whys, but in the midst of my whys I find Him. He is the answer to the *why*! I still trust Him!

***W**ith*
***H**ope*
***Y**ielded*

Treasures I Found in the Dark

If we can see God as the God of the Bible, sovereign, supreme, sensitive, not allowing death and trials except by divine permission, then we can see purpose, even if we don't know what that purpose is.

We must grow through the sadness. We must change—not because we want to, but because we choose to. I am not and will never be the same person. I am forever changed by my loss— my son's departure. Some changes have been good, and I can smile; other changes are not what I asked for, so I try to smile through them. In God's grace He has helped me to embrace the new me. I have given Him complete reign over my life to do what He desires. He did not do a remodel but a whole demolition.

We were determined that our misery would be used for God's ministry. Before Dustan went to heaven we had all made a promise to one another. No matter what we had been through and no matter what our lives held for the future, we were no longer going to put God in a box. We knew that all things were possible with God (Matthew 19:26) as long as our own expectations did not hold Him back.

Our God box was getting ready to explode.

We had a lot of true beliefs that were only beliefs. Our hearts weren't there. Instead of just checking off the Christian checklist we needed to know God's unconditional love; to be a part of God's healing; to be able to share God's love with others. We knew we served a God who was able to do all that we asked, and that He promised. We just had lost that connection of feeling His closeness. We had faith in God but had lost the ability to see His love for us. We had gotten comfortable with our Christianity and had forgotten about the most important part, which was our relationship with Him.

One morning I was journaling and telling the Lord how the last several years had been so excruciating without Dustan. I felt like I was all alone and that He had even pulled back His blessings from me. As I began to write I almost could not keep up with the words that were spilling onto my paper.

RESTING IN HIM

My Dear Child,
Yes, it seems that I have pulled back my blessings, because you were confusing my blessings with my love for you.

Yes—I bless you because I love you; but my blessings are not my love. I needed you to see me for who I truly am, "LOVE," not attached to anything, BUT just Love. Because of love I do all these things for you, but I do not love you because of these things. For you to love my people you must see them for truly who they are, not what they can give you. You are to give them my love, and how can you give them my love without understanding what my love is? My love is pure and holy. I love because I am love. I am always with you so I always love you. You cannot measure my love by what I do or do not do or what I give or do not give you. I love because I am!

I want you to know my love for what it is—ME! Feel ME, know ME, and recognize ME. Don't look at me with ideas or things. My love is just knowing, not having. I don't pull my love back from you at any time. I always love you because I am always with you.

That seed of love was planted, painfully; now it has started to blossom and grow. As it grows in your heart it pushes everything out that does not belong there, even man-made love. Yes, it can be painful, but that's not because I want it to be; it is because you make it to be. You hold onto things that don't belong in your new heart of love—my heart. As long as you hang onto them, the more I love the harder it is for my love to fill your heart. With those things still there, they cramp the flourishing new growth.

If you freely let go of them, my love can fill your heart so quickly and painlessly that you will never know you are in the process of preparation.

STOP dwelling on the growth and embrace the process! Why do you love Dustan?

Treasures I Found in the Dark

(My Reply)
He is a part of me, and my son. He did not earn my love—he just received it because he was a part of me. Part of who I am was living in Dustan's heart. Because of that we had a heart connection, a bond of love. It is the same with God and me. I am a part of Him now. We have a bond of love, a heart connection.

April,
My love must be enough. In reality it is enough, but you must see and feel that it is enough. When you do then all other relationships will become fuller. You will not be looking for them to fill you up and meet a need. Because you will already be filled with me—LOVE!! Oh, my child, embrace me and you will be overwhelmed with me—LOVE!!!

He met me that morning when I needed to know that someone cared and loved me with a love that I never knew existed, because the love I had been experiencing just did not seem to be enough. He showed me more of Himself so in return I could show Him to others.

In the darkness you can barely function. You walk slowly, one step at a time, reaching out for anything to steady and guide you until you can see the light. When you find the light you reach your hand forward so that you can walk together in the same direction. The light is your heavenly Father, the Truth. Once you grab hold of the Truth you can walk hand in hand knowing you are in His perfect will for your life. What a treasure I have found while I stumbled in the darkness.

It took my letting go of Dustan here on earth to experience true life. My son ultimately gave me life. I thought it was the other way around. I gave life to him on May 7, 1990, and he lived for eighteen years with me. When he passed from earth to heaven he left me LIFE. His passing taught me the real meaning of God's life—his abundant life. I thought I knew what living life in Christ really was until Christ was all I had. Then I realized you don't experience life until you experience death, your own death to yourself—your desires, your dreams, and your wants. Dying to self has taught me a freedom I have never known before: freedom from the bondages of this world, freedom from religion, freedom from myself. All these things kept me from living in complete reliance on my Father.

This was my journey to dying to self, and Christ exchanging his life for mine. The phrase "the exchanged life" was foreign to me until September 2009, when I enrolled in a discipleship program through Grace Ministries of Tennessee. I truly believe God led me to GMT to teach me about His grace, forgiveness, and most importantly His love. Even after hearing these words and the definition, it has taken me years to truly understand what the exchanged life means. Now I not only know what it means, I live every moment of my life knowing that Christ truly exchanged His life for mine.

What does this mean, exchanged His life? In his booklet "Resolving Misunderstandings of the Exchanged Life," Professor John Best describes it simply as our union with Christ in His death, burial, resurrection, and ascension. He goes on to say that,

> ...at the moment of our salvation, God took us out of spiritual death in Adam and transformed us into union with Christ. He exchanged our old identity as sinners in Adam for a radically new identity in Christ. We are now not just sinners saved by grace; our essential nature and identity is that of new creation, saints in Christ. Our union with Christ is so real, so vital, so complete, so transhistorical that the old us (our spirit) in Adam died, and was buried. The new us (our spiritual identity) is now raised up in union with Jesus. We have been set free to live as ones who have been recreated in Christ's resurrection.

My first thoughts when I read this were, Umm! That sounds good. Christ gave me *His* life. Did I really know what this meant? No! I had always been taught simply that Christ died for my sins, which in itself is pretty amazing; but to think—when

Treasures I Found in the Dark

He died on the cross it was so that He would have the opportunity to come dwell inside me, that I would be used as a vessel for His light and glory to be shown. Now that is what I call exchanging His life for mine.

I would like to describe my personal journey of experiencing the true exchanged life. Reading the definition is great, but God showing me what it meant had much more impact on me. Let me just be honest, the last couple of years I have been in a spiritual pit. I did not mean for it to happen; it just did, right? That is what we always say when we do not want to admit that we had a choice, and I chose to be in that pit. I admit it. I chose it.

"Pity, table for one?" Yep, that is my table. A quiet table in the dark corner, please. No, do not join me. This is my party. I push all the chairs away except mine. I sit alone at my table. People visit, but I do not ask them to sit with me. They may actually say things I NEED to hear. I do not want that. I want to dwell on what I want to believe is truth. My truth as I see it!

As I sit watching others enjoy life, laughing with one another, I indulge in thoughts like: *Man, grass sure is greener on the other side. Why me, Lord? Why did this happen to me, why my son, why my family? Did you not get it? I cannot live without him. I said, I cannot do it! Were you not listening? I told you over and over, I cannot do it!*

Then just when I think I am alone at my table for one, I hear my heavenly Father say, "I know you cannot, but I can." *Okay fine YOU do it! I give up.*

That still small voice inside says, "Finally! I have been waiting for you to give up, April! You cannot do it. But if you give it to me I can do it through you."

While sitting at my table for one, I thought I was thinking about my son, believing life would be better if he were here with me, believing my way was better than my

RESTING IN HIM

Father's way, and believing in me and not my Father. That was a mistake. It wasn't about my son at all. It was about me. Yes, me, me, and me.

The "exchanged life" has changed my view of my Christian walk. I see now that it's not about me or my dreams. It is all about Him and His dreams for me. It is about dying to self (my flesh) so that His Spirit (His life) can be lived through me.

For me to truly understand the exchanged life I would have to understand His unconditional love. If I was going to choose to let His Spirit live through me then I would need to experience my true intimate relationship with my Father, the love I so desired and craved.

My heart was broken and my spirit was crushed. I had come to a place where I must surrender all. It was in this place that the Father knew He could finally teach me that in myself I can do nothing, but in Him I can do all things. The truth was that He loved me so unconditionally that He not only gave His life for my sins, He also wanted to make sure that I would live victoriously here on earth. How is that possible? The answer is "the exchanged life." Everything that He is, I am.

Watchman Nee tells a story of a young brother in his book *The Normal Christian Life* that conveys the meaning of "You can do nothing apart from Christ" (John 15:5). In the story Watchman Nee asks this young brother, who is young in years but mature in the Lord,

> "Brother, what has the Lord really been teaching you these days?"
> He replied, "Only one thing: that I can do nothing apart from him."
> "Do you really mean," I asked, "that you can do nothing?"
> "Well, no," he said. "Of course I can do many things! In fact that has been my trouble. Oh, you know, I have always been so confident in myself. I know I am able to do a lot of things."

So I asked, "What then do you mean when you say you can do nothing apart from him?"

He answered, "The Lord has shown me that I can do anything, but that he has said, 'Apart from me ye can do nothing.' So it comes to this, that everything I have done and can still do apart from him is just that… NOTHING!"

This is what began to ring true in my life. I was doing a lot of things, but it really was just nothing and I was going nowhere.

When I started to live by the exchanged life concept, several things occurred. One, I noticed the battle of flesh and spirit. This battle had already been raging, I just did not know it had already been won. Knowing the battle was won changed the way I looked at everything I did, every decision I made, and how I lived out my Christian walk.

Secondly, I began to realize that God did not love me because of what I did or did not do. He loved me because I was His and He is Love.

Thirdly, I was not bound to religion but was in a relationship with a Father who adored me. In *A Divine Invitation*, author Steve McVey says, "The Bible isn't an instruction manual. It's a love letter with personalized notes to each of us that can only be really seen as the Holy Spirit shows them to us." He describes "prayer as a supernatural and mystical action by which two lovers whisper to each other. Church life is a kingdom party where we come to the dance and celebrate this unbelievably rich life He has given us— at no cost to us whatsoever." How beautifully stated. You mean it was not a demand and obligation that I read my Bible, pray, and go to church? These are things that God gives me for myself—not for Him. "God loves me so much he wants to deliver me from the misery of MUST into the triumph of TRUST."

God knew something that I did not! He knew that I could make it through *with Him*. He knew I would seek Him until I found Him.

RESTING IN HIM

One of my favorite readings, as previously mentioned, from my *Hinds' Feet* devotional, hit me like a ton of bricks the first time I read it, and I go back to it often; it solidifies the concept of dying to my flesh/myself. I will repeat this quote: "Losing one's life is painful. It's death! Upon hearing a missionary's report of God's work, a woman commented, 'I'd give my life to be used like that!' The missionary replied, 'That's what it would cost!'"

Every day I have to remind myself to look from God's perspective, not mine, and then I die.

For so many years I walked in semi-darkness, blind to the truth of God's love. I believed he would love me only if I did all the right things, if I accomplished my daily checklist of religious works. I saw the cross as a ritual or requirement of Jesus: God sent Him to die for us—He was required to do so. As the truth of God's unconditional love started to sink deep down in my heart, I realized He chose to die on the cross. Love sent Him there and love kept Him there until it was finished. He gave His life so that you and I could have ours for eternity. What a beautiful love story.

His Spirit reveals this truth to us as He brings us to the point where we can begin to grasp it. When we realize His life was exchanged for ours we will be able to live an overcoming life. Then we stop striving to do life on our own; once we realize who we are—our true identity—that "as he is so also are we in this world" (I John 4:17, ESV), we then become who we were always meant to be: overcomers! This may be a lifetime journey, but I am willing to take it with my Father.

I am often reminded of the light that caused Paul to become helpless in himself: "As he neared Damascus on his journey, suddenly a light from heaven flashed around him" (Acts 9:3, NIV). Paul was blinded by the light. For three days he was blind and his friends led him around. I believe that shining light and his blindness prepared him for the dark prison he was about to experience. He was brought to a place where he could do little but fast and pray. I am sure he turned his sight inward to look at the truth of what he was doing, persecuting Jesus. While I was walking in my darkness, I, too, saw the light. It was not a shining light, but a life-changing light. It was the beautiful sparkle of his love and truth.

Treasures Found in the Darkness:

I found a true intimate relationship with Christ and His unconditional love.

Healing is not forgetting, but it is remembering with love, tenderness, and joy the life you shared with your loved one.

I realized the Bible is not only the road map for my life but it's like a traveling companion for my journey, Jesus' heavenly hand to hold along the way.

He will use my darkness to reflect His light.

His truth.

Every day is a gift; I learned not to take it for granted.

God calls each of us to light for another the flame once extinguished by despair.

Dustan is a far greater part of my future than he is of my past.

I found a reflection of my true self, Jesus.

RESTING IN HIM

This quote accompanied me on my journey to the depths of grief, "You never know how much you really believe anything until its truth or falsehood becomes a matter of life and death to you." (C.S. Lewis)

The dark does not destroy the light;
it defines it. It's our fear of the dark that casts our joy
into the shadows.
—BRENÉ BROWN

People are like stained-glass windows.
They sparkle and shine when the sun is out,
but when the darkness sets in their beauty is revealed
only if there is a light from within.
—ELISABETH KUBLER-ROSS

Because of the tender mercy of our God,
with which the Sunrise from on high will visit us,
to shine upon those who sit in darkness and the shadow
of death, to guide our feet into the way of peace.
(LUKE 1:78,79, NASB)

The light shines in the darkness,
and the darkness can never extinguish it.
(JOHN 1:15, NLT)

Treasures I Found in the Dark

CHAPTER 12

It's a God Thing

*While we're obsessed with the here and now,
God is focused on forever.*
—LIZ HIGGS

In February 2008 Dustan had written about his cancer journey for a school paper:

Early October in the year 2005 I was diagnosed with leukemia, and after that my life would be changed forever. When this happened I was just starting my sophomore year at school and found out that I would not be back at school for the rest of the year. This news really struck my family hard. But afterwards we pulled together as a family. We decided that we would not let this hinder us and we would fight this horrible disease. I started all my chemotherapy, and in two weeks the doctors announced that I was in remission. Just because I was in remission that doesn't mean the hard part is over. It was actually just beginning.

RESTING IN HIM

Throughout the first year of chemotherapy everything was going pretty smoothly. I was doing my schoolwork by some homeschooling books, and my teachers would come to my house to help with the rest. During this first year my mom and I would go to the clinic once a week for my chemotherapy. Because of chemotherapy I was not able to go anywhere except the house and the clinic.

We were ending the first year of chemotherapy and everything was going fine, when all of a sudden one day at home I started to have a seizure. When this happened my mom called the ambulance and they took me to the hospital. I got to the hospital and started to have another one. When I woke up from the second seizure I was hooked to all these heart monitors. When you're fifteen years old—everything is going through your mind; this was probably the scariest moment of my life besides the fact I had leukemia. When the doctors came and saw me, they said these seizures were caused by the chemotherapy.

Finally I went home from all this. But it wasn't even a week later, half my body went numb; this turned out to be a minor stroke. Once again the doctors said it was caused by the chemotherapy.

Probably the biggest thing that happened to me that first year of treatment was that one of the drugs I was taking for chemotherapy stayed in my body too long and burned the inside of my body. I spent at least a month and a half in the hospital trying to get better. The doctors told us they had never seen this before. They were shocked; it was very abnormal for this to happen.

Since this was abnormal, one of my doctors was documenting everything that happened and what they did to fix the problems. Well, it turns out not even two months later, after I was better and at home, some girl in Florida had the same thing happen to her. So my doctor heard about this and sent what he had documented about me to Florida. This helped the girl heal faster because they knew exactly what to do.

It's a God Thing

The second year of chemotherapy was very easy because all the hard drugs had been done. So now it was just monthly visits to the clinic. At this time I was a junior. I was able to go to school, but I still missed a lot of classes because of visits to the clinic, and occasionally getting sick. When you have leukemia, whenever you get sick you have to stay in the hospital for a couple of days.

Starting my third and final year of chemotherapy, I was excited and ready; it was my senior year and I was set to enjoy this year. But when October of 2007 came, I was shocked to find out the leukemia was back. When the doctor told me and my family, it shook me up. I only had one more year left of treatment; and, what really hurt the most—this was my senior year. The doctors told me that this time around I would have to have a bone marrow transplant.

A bone marrow transplant is where they take certain cells from a donor who matches me, and transfuse those cells into me. It's like somebody giving me a new immune system. So the doctors had my mom, dad, and brother tested to see if they were matches. The doctor told us that most likely one of them would be a match. It turned out that my brother was a 100% match.

He was excited and so was I. My brother, Dylan, was excited he could help me fight this again; because last time, all he could do was sit there and watch me be in pain. So I was excited for him.

Well here I am now, about two weeks from my transplant and a couple of months from graduating. Throughout my whole high school experience, I have had only one full year of school, and that was my freshmen year. After freshman year, I missed a whole lot, or was not there at all. So I am looking forward to college. When I graduate from high school I will attend Volunteer State Community College while I am doing my last bit of treatment, but after that I am going to Trevecca University.

RESTING IN HIM

After enduring all this these past three years, I have decided to become a counselor or a therapist. I want to help teenagers who are going through really hard times in their lives, as I did.

Through these past three years my friends, newspaper reporters, family members, and all sorts of people have asked me, How are you so calm through all of this, and how do you always have a positive attitude toward everything? The answer is, both times they told me I had leukemia, I was scared (and for some reason, deep down inside me I knew I had it before the doctors found it both times); but even though I was sad, I decided to accept it and move on. You cannot sit there and dwell upon what is going to happen.

You have to look towards the future, because if you sit there and dwell upon it you will make yourself miserable and sick. Just always have a positive attitude toward everything and don't ask why. Just say okay and move on.
Dustan Gammon

My son's words pierce my soul every time I read them. How can such a young man have such wisdom? The only answer is the power of the cross. When Christ gave His life for those who choose to be His children He gave everything we would ever need. For Dustan and our family, we needed everything through this journey; and our everything was JESUS!!!

From the moment God started preparing us for the cancer journey until the last words written in this book, it has been heart-aching, heart-breaking, heart-shattering, heart-stopping, heart-loving, heart-warming, but most of all heart-changing.

God prepared our hearts to be able to travel the journey, to overcome our broken dreams, to find our rope of hope, to experience true brotherly love with our brothers and sisters in Christ, to recognize the true miracles in our lives, to know fully what was, what is, and what will be, to understand when to take a step out of the boat

It's a God Thing

and when to rest with Him in the boat, to withstand the ultimate sacrifice of death for life, to feel God's presence in the healing process, and to see His light shine through our darkness.

Is it a God thing? Absolutely, it is. Romans 8:26–30 in The Message translation states it this way,

> Meanwhile, the moment we get tired in the waiting, God's Spirit is right alongside helping us along. If we don't know how or what to pray, it doesn't matter. He does our praying in and for us, making prayer out of our wordless sighs, our aching groans. He knows us far better than we know ourselves, knows our pregnant condition, and keeps us present before God. That's why we can be so sure that every detail in our lives of love for God is worked into something good. God knew what he was doing from the very beginning. He decided from the outset to shape the lives of those who love him along the same lines as the life of his Son. The Son stands first in the line of humanity he restored. We see the original and intended shape of our lives there in him. After God made that decision of what his children should be like, he followed it up by calling people by name. After he called them by name, he set them on a solid basis with himself. And then, after getting them established, he stayed with them to the end, gloriously completing what he had begun.

Dustan and I had talked and dreamed about writing a book together. It was to be called *A Mother and Son's Journey Through Cancer*. On many occasions we talked about all the things that would be written and how our struggles could hopefully help someone else during their cancer journey. The days after he passed I knew that dream too had died. Oh, but my heavenly Father knew better. He had a plan all along. When I thought my dream had died, I laid it at His feet. He resurrected a new dream. A book was to be written, but it was not about our story; it was about His glory, where He was in the midst of Dustan's cancer, Dustan's death, our grief, and most importantly our journey to finding joy again.

RESTING IN HIM

As you can imagine Jesus and I have had many conversations over the years, some intense, some one-sided, but most of them very comfortable and intimate. One of those conversations pertained to this book. I reminded Him of all the things I felt I was not capable of doing, such as writing a book. He reminded me that I can do all things through Him who gives me strength. He's not looking for capability but availability. I then reminded Him that I would have to be vulnerable and share my most intimate thoughts. He knew that was not me. I would have to put myself out there for people to see the real me. He knew I would struggle with that. I then would have to share the one thing that I never thought I would or could: my true heart. He knew my heart had been tucked away for safekeeping. I then would have to lay my heart out for everyone to see its rawness and its wounds. He knew I would shrink in terror. Writing every word on these pages has caused me to open my heart; so He was able to caress, mold, heal, and fill every hole left by the many hurts in my life.

He knew it was a God thing. He knew all along that healing would come. He knew—and that's why I know I can *Rest in Him*, because He knows.

After riding that Ugly Monster roller-coaster and then being thrown into the House of Mirrors I still can find rest in Him, because I know He is still with me—that He lives in me. I remember when I would look in those mirrors searching for truth, what looked back at me was scary. It was not the real April. It was the one who had learned to smile through all life's hurts, the one who had been taught her words were not important, and the one whose heart had been beaten and bruised beyond recognition. The one the world had created. The longer I gazed in that mirror the more in focus my image became. Slowly and over time I started to see the real April. The mask I had been wearing started to crumble. God was starting to reveal the beauty of my own face. As I started putting foundation on, the word of God in my heart, those blemishes became my beauty marks.

Day after day I would ask that mirror, "Mirror, mirror, on the wall, who is the truest of them all?"

It's a God Thing

I could let that mirror define who I thought I was—broken, bruised, unworthy, rejected, unlovable, or I could let that still small voice speak truth to my heart. You are loved, accepted, worthy, healed, and made whole.

The words spoken to us over our lifetime by family, friends, spouse, co-workers, and others can cause the same effect as our distorted mirror. We begin to believe the words spoken over us are our true identity. Then when we look in the mirror we see who the world has created, not who Christ says we are. In Genesis 1:26, we have been created in the image and likeness of God; therefore, we must begin to see ourselves the way God sees us.

As my wounded heart was exposed, Christ began to reveal to me my real heart—His heart. James 1:23,24 says, "For if anyone is a hearer of the word and not a doer, he is like a man who looks at his natural face in a mirror; for once he has looked at himself and gone away, he has immediately forgotten what kind of person he was" (NASB).

James is telling us that God's word is like a mirror reflecting our true image: our true selves—Christ. So as I began to put His word in my heart, His heart became my heart. His face became my face. I was seeing for the first time my true image.

I hid behind my mask for more years than I like to admit, until one day my mask began to break. All my pain was causing cracks in my self-made mask; but the beauty of that was, God's light/love started to shine through those cracks. His love began to slowly let the mask slip from my face. Then the true beauty, His love and truth, began to show on my face.

You see, He knew. He knew by my exposing my wounded heart, both I and others, as well, would find healing. Yes, it's a God thing. My one prayer through Dustan's death would be that only good would come from it. I can honestly say, as hard as this journey has been, we have purposely focused and moved toward the good.

RESTING IN HIM

In writing this book I had to travel back through the days of cancer diagnosis, treatments, hospital stays, ravaging effects of chemotherapy, unexpected miracles, blessings, new friendships, high school days, relapses, graduations, DEATH, broken dreams, excruciating pain of loss, new normal, grace, more loss, unspeakable joy, and restoration. My journals have been my best friends for the last ten years. They in themselves are a book written back to me where I can see the fingerprints of God in the midst of all my days. Not one page written was without a conversation with my one true love, the one who never judged me, condemned me, or walked away from me. He loved, He listened, He led, He corrected, He comforted, and most importantly, He never left.

After Dustan passed it was very important for me to have pictures all around. That is my nature anyway, but I went to the extreme. I knew all I had left were pictures of his sweet precious face and I wanted to be reminded always of him. (As if my heart did not already remind me.) It was so difficult to take family photos after his death. It was like a dagger in my heart. There was always something missing in the picture. Reluctantly, I took them, but I would tuck them away, not to be reminded of our new normal.

Then one day out of the blue, God whispered to my heart, "April, it is time. It is time for you to get those pictures of you three and put them out." So I went through our house and took all the pictures and put them on the floor. I cried, I screamed, and I laughed. It was time.

I went to my box and got all the pictures of Kenny, Dylan, and me, and placed them beside all the others. I reminisced about all the good, bad, and ugly times. Then I chose all my favorites, framed them, and placed them around the house.

For some, this may not seem very big. For me, it was huge. It was accepting that this is what our life really is, the three of us; and you know, it was okay. I was okay. What I noticed as the commonality of all the pictures was our smiles. Our

It's a God Thing

smiles were genuine before Dustan's death and after. We may not have been in the happiest of circumstances, but we had joy in every picture. That's a God thing.

I found a special treasure while putting away the leftover photos. There was a picture of our family of four our first Christmas after Dustan's diagnosis in October. Dustan's t-shirt said, "AIRAPOSTLE" across the top and, "1 Thessalonians 4:16–17" at the bottom. Now mind you I had looked at this picture literally thousands of times. That day I stopped and really looked at it, then I decided to look up the scripture. Let me just say my hands could not go up fast enough to praise and thank God. Beside me I had a God's Word Translation praying Bible, and this is how it read:

Comfort About Christians Who Have Died

Brothers and sisters, we don't want you to be ignorant about those who have died. We don't want you to grieve like other people who have no hope. We believe that Jesus died and came back to life. We also believe that, through Jesus, God will bring back those who have died. They will come back with Jesus. We are telling you what the Lord taught. We who are still alive when the Lord comes will not go into his kingdom ahead of those who have already died. The Lord will come from heaven with a command, with the voice of the archangel, and with the trumpet call of God. First, the dead who believed in Christ will come back to life. Then, together with them, we who are still alive will be taken in the clouds to meet the Lord in the air. In this way we will always be with the Lord. So then, comfort each other with these words.

RESTING IN HIM

Really!? You tell me God is not in the smallest of details of our lives. His timing is perfect. He knew at that moment I was trying to accept that our new family photos would only be of us three. He let me know that Dustan was perfectly fine. He had made it to his ultimate destination and we would be united again.

As part of my healing I would write Dustan a letter every month, then after a couple of years it became only on those special occasions: his birthday, Mother's Day, Father's Day, the anniversary of his death, etc. I read these now to see the progression of my acceptance that he was in heaven and not with me. One in particular let me know that I was coming to accept my reality.

June 28, 2015
Seventh anniversary of his death.

Dustan—
Today is the day...the day you left me here on earth so that you could be in the presence of Jesus. I still have mixed emotions. I mean, what kind of mother would I be <u>NOT</u> to want you here with me; although actually I really want to be the mother who is so thrilled that you are walking with Jesus. I could never ask for you to come back—NEVER! You are surrounded by ALL that is good, and overwhelmed with LOVE. I really cannot explain or even begin to imagine ALL that you are experiencing now. But, even with the little that I think I know, it is enough never to ask or hope for you to come back. We are surrounded by all that is evil in this world. With that being said—I have ALL that is good living in me, so even though evil abounds good seeps from me. Yay, God!

Can you see me? I wonder. I was told that when we do things here on earth for the glory of God, ALL in heaven can see us and they rejoice. So do you rejoice when I follow my divine destiny: to speak God's truth to others? And when I show God's love to a hurting world?

It's a God Thing

I want to do all these things because of the love I have for my Father, but to know you see me and we have a connection from the earth to heaven makes my heart leap out of my chest. WOW!!!

When I praise, I believe that's when Spirit meets flesh. When I praise the Lord, does your spirit connect with my spirit? I sure hope so!

Absence truly makes the heart grow fonder. I miss you more and more each day. I love you, sweet one, more than words can describe. Yet, I cannot even find words that are sufficient. I have to admit life here can be so stinking hard. Others seem to enjoy it so much more than I. Me—I realize we were never meant to live here and be comfortable enough to stay. This is not my home!

Who better to know that than you? I only wish I could see you in your home. What does it look like, what are you doing, who are you with, what are you thinking? I am naïve enough to think you miss me, but truly I know you have ALL you need — JESUS!

He is the one our hearts crave and desire anyways. So it is only natural for you to be complete and whole where you are, as much as I miss you and would love to have you here with me. I know the truth! You are in the BEST place ever. I have to admit I am a little envious on some days that I still am here and you are not.

On another note…. I am still writing our book. I have the hardest time moving forward with it, because it was our project together. I remember our conversations; so don't worry, they will be included like you wanted. When our book is complete it will be as if I have to say goodbye to you again. So as each page gets closer to the end I find it harder to finish my thoughts.

Sometimes I wonder will I always write you letters. Will it ever stop? Somehow I think it would be like our conversations have ended. I don't think I could allow that.

RESTING IN HIM

I love you, sweetness, and miss you more that my pen can write.

I love you from here to there and back again.
Love, Mom

My letters to Dustan have been great therapy for me. It's been a way for me to have conversations with him and to be able to still write out his name. That was another loss I had to grieve, just saying his name in conversations. You do not realize how much less his name is said until you do not hear it. I usually chuckle when writing his letters because in the many conversations we had he would listen, nod, and smile. What a wonderful counselor he would have made. So in some sense my letters are the same as were our conversations.

I loved that blue-eyed, blonde-haired, tenderhearted, wisdom-speaking boy of mine. He was a beautiful brave soul. He loved life and lived every day as if it were his last. He gave his talents and gifts back to the Lord in his music and sweet angelic voice. Always there with a helping hand, a wise word, and big smile. His giggle would make everyone laugh out loud.

It has been ten years this month that he left earth. I miss him more and more as each day passes. The good thing is, every day is a day closer until we reunite again.

It's a God thing.... Tears flow so freely down my face as I share these thoughts with you. I know God has a plan. I know Kenny, Dylan, and I are different people now. We will never be the same. This is not necessarily bad. If we stay the same old people we will get the same old results. You see, we have been put through the refiner's fire. We are being shaped just as He wants us to be. We must yield to His molding and His shaping. He uses His hands in love while changing us one stroke at a time. I want to be different. I want to be just like Him. I am not who I used to be, but I am still not who He wants me to be. I will continue to change for Him.

It's a God Thing

I am excited about the possibilities and all the new opportunities that I have in Him. I am choosing to walk each day with Him hand in hand. Maybe with this new season I won't spend the entire time on my knees, but God will let my knees heal. Then I will be standing tall with my hands raised towards a place that I long to be my home, my Heaven.

Several months after Dustan had passed I sent out the following message to all the many people who had been following our story. I wanted them all to know the impact they had made on our lives. That was such a God thing, that they chose to follow our journey through cancer. Without this community of people we surely would have vanished under our grief. Sometimes God gives us the answer before we know the question. He also will place people in our paths before we even know we need them. Only He can do that.

I want to start off this new beginning by saying: Thank you! Without each of you and all of your prayers, gifts, and love we would have been just another family struck by tragedy. A family lost within this worldly system. You, my brothers and sisters in Christ, have stood this test right along with us. You have made a huge impact on our lives and in our Christian walk. I am so glad I am among family that, while not sharing the same last name, share the same Father. We all have the same goal, to love one another just as our Father loves us.

Will my thoughts continue to be shared in the future? Only God knows. Maybe He chose for me to use this as a stepping stone for my future. All I know is that it's not my thoughts but His that I want to share. If any of you knew me before this journey then you knew I was a very private person who never shared my thoughts. So I raise my hands to my Father and lift my eyes from the keyboard and say, Your will be done not mine.

Dustan taught me a lot of things. One of the most important is that, like Peter, you must step out of the boat. You must have the faith to know that your Father

RESTING IN HIM

will meet you wherever you are. He taught me about hope. Hope in his Father's promises. This is what he put in his senior yearbook:

FAVORITE SCRIPTURE:
Jeremiah 29:11,
'For I know the plans I have for you,' declares the Lord, 'plans to prosper you and not to harm you, plans to give you hope and a future' (NIV).

FAVORITE QUOTE:
One Life…One Chance!

He lived this out right before our very eyes. May we all start each new day with these same thoughts. Thank you, Dustan. I love you from the bottom of my heart, which means forever, because you took the bottom of my heart with you.

Remember we are BLESSED: Boundlessly Loved Extravagantly Saved Supplied Empowered and Delivered.

I leave you with this:

We often see ourselves as fragile, breakable souls. We live in fear of that which we are certain we can't survive. As children of God, we are only as fragile as our unwillingness to turn and hide our face in Him. Our pride alone is fragile. Once its shell is broken and the heart is laid bare, we can sense the caress of God's tender care. Until then, He holds us just the same.

Resting in Him as he changes us one stroke of His hand at a time,
April, Kenny, Dylan, and in memory of Dustan

Today I am thankful for new beginnings and unexpected miracles.

It's a God Thing

She could never go back and make some of the details pretty. All she could do was move forward and make the whole beautiful.

—TERRI ST. CLOUD

Dylan's wedding day, May 5, 2018

CHAPTER 13

The Number Thirty-One

For I will turn their mourning into joy.
I will comfort them
and exchange their sorrow for rejoicing.
(JEREMIAH 31:13, NLT)

Below is a letter I wrote to Dustan in December 2016. Christmas was always so difficult for us. The year Dustan passed away we started a new tradition, so as to keep him a part of our holiday. We would each write a letter to the other, even Dustan. We would place those letters in our stockings to be read after a busy day of festivities, when the house was quiet and our minds had come to rest. We would each read our letters alone. The letters were to include moments throughout the year that meant the most to us. We made sure to include an encouragement or memory that stood out to us. We also would write what we were looking forward to in the upcoming year. This was our way of saying those things that we might forget to say during the year. We wanted our Christmas to be enjoyable, not sad.

RESTING IN HIM

To My Dear Precious 31,
I miss you. Not one single day goes by that I do not think of you, that I do not feel your sweetness and beauty in my life. That I do not linger on saying your name or gazing at your photo.

We moved! That was hard, leaving our house where you lived with us and where we spent our last moments together. So hard! It was time. At least, that's what we felt God was leading us to. Sometimes I wonder, but I do trust Him. I will try to follow your example of faith and love without wavering. You did do it so well; me, I still have my days.

I've moved on in life but the great thing is I took you with me. Always you will go with me.

You are in my heart, my memories, but most of all in Dylan. I see you a lot in him and it makes me smile. You would have been so proud of him. He is doing great things with a great God! Oh, what a journey for him!

This year as we celebrate Christmas—Jesus' birth—I am even more thankful because you now live with Him. Because He lives—you too live, and we will see each other again.

I wrote this letter as a goodbye to our home/house...

> *Yesterday, as we walked out these doors for the last time, we smiled, we cried—our hearts a little lighter. We have packed so many boxes of material things, every little item nestled in its rightful place, wrapped securely so it will be protected as we transition to our new destination. In the same way as the material things, we have packed ever so carefully all our memories, also: the bad, the good, the ugly, and the precious, in a neat little box of our hearts. As we close these doors, let go of the*

The Number Thirty-One

doorknob, and walk down each step as a family of three, we will always be a family of four—no matter what doors we walk through.

At the end of the day this is just a house. Walls built by men brick by brick.

We are thankful wherever we go, Our Home, built by us memory by memory, goes with us. We leave nothing behind.

When our cars leave the driveway and we take that last turn through our neighborhood we know one thing for sure. We loved, we laughed, and, OH, how we lived. We will miss all the sweet people who inhabited these houses that led to our safe place in the world.

How do you say goodbye to a place so dear to your heart? You don't. You gaze upon the beauty of each treasured moment and take that next step to make new memories as you walk through that new door.

RESTING IN HIM

After establishing the Christmas letter tradition, we learned a very important lesson. The best gift we can give someone is our words. Words are a gift that keeps on giving. These letters have become my most treasured gifts. All the letters written to Dustan have been put away for safekeeping. Someday when the time is right we will pull these letters out and read them. If not, I pray they will be treasured keepsakes for the generations to come.

Just like leaving our house that we inhabited for ten years, we had learned to leave our sadness behind. It was time to let our mourning turn into gladness. As we left our painful past behind us we gathered together to talk about what we had learned over the last years. One of the most visible was the peace we had experienced from the moment Dustan had been diagnosed even up to the present. The peace that the world cannot give you. Philippians 4:7, "the peace of God, which surpasses all understanding, will guard your hearts and your minds in Christ Jesus" (ESV).

No matter what road we had traveled, straight, curvy, solid, sinking, or even the dead ends, this peace never left us. It did guard our hearts and minds. It kept us from sinking to the place of no return.

This peace created a bond between us three that no one could ever break. This peace created a wholeness and wellness abiding inside of us, rising from our faith in Christ Jesus. Kenny and I beat the odds of becoming another statistic of a divorced couple who had dealt with the loss of a child. We became stronger together. We pulled each other close and never let go. We played the see-saw game on many occasions. He was up and I was down and vice versa. Our faith in God was the board we were sitting on.

God was so faithful, and eventually we learned to balance together and to accept the ride. Dylan had to slay his own Ugly Monster. He journeyed through the valley of the shadow of death and walked out on the other side as a shining light. His is the pure light of one who can overcome. He found his own relationship with Jesus.

The Number Thirty-One

He found the one who would complete him. He no longer looked for things to help him cope or satisfy. He had found the one his true heart desired; it was Jesus!

Now the number 31 is not spiritual in any way. I just know that God uses this number to show us time and time again that Dustan is ever with us. God is always in the details—the smallest of details.

The number 31 was Dustan's number when he played little league sports; and then it followed him throughout high school. Even though he was unable to play in high school because of his illness, Mt. Juliet Christian Academy still made No. 31 his number. MJCA retired this number when Dustan passed and it now represents his legacy. It was painted with angel wings above the gym door where the basketball players enter before each game. Each player would jump and touch the 31 to remember to "Never Give Up," and you have "One Life One Chance" to make a difference and to give everything you've got.

The number still lives on throughout our lives today. The impact:
- He had 32 seniors in his graduating class. When he passed it left 31 students.
- He fought the cancer battle for 31 months; in the 32nd month he won the battle.
- Dustan's number is 31 and Dylan's number is 13. He passed at 1:31 p.m. on June 28, 2008.
- His plot in the Savior's Garden, which was purchased in 1970, was plot No. 31.
- He is buried next to my mom, whose birthday is the first day of March (3/1).
- We released 31 balloons at his gravesite when he was buried. Thirty-one different people held them; yet all balloons floated back together in the sky and stayed together as though one.
- Our first Thanksgiving without him we took a last-minute trip to Miss Patti's Settlement in Kentucky. The interstate exit just happens to be 31.
- My dad's exit to his house is exit 31, New Hope Road.
- A devotion found by Dustan's bedside:

RESTING IN HIM

Day Thirty-One: NEVER, NEVER, NEVER GIVE UP.
Winners are just ex-losers who got mad.
The battle belongs to the persistent.
The victory will go to the one who never quits.
Refuse to let circumstance defeat you.
From the ashes of defeat burn the greatest fires of accomplishment.
God made you to climb, not crawl.
God made you to fly, not fall.
God made you to soar, not sink.
You were made to soar the clouds with the WINGS OF AN EAGLE!
THE WORD FOR WINNERS: "I can do all things through Christ who strengthens me." (Philippians 4:13, KJ2000)

That was Dustan's motto, "Never give up." His last entry in his journal talks about his journey through cancer. There are several statements he writes that remind me what faith he had in God. The most powerful is how he views God even after going through those horrible years on the Ugly Monster. In his own words:

> *I think about what all I have gone through and it just blows my mind that God has been so good to me. People always say, "Why, God? Why me?" That's usually what people say when bad things happen. Actually, I remember on October 5, 2005, when I was diagnosed I can remember saying that. But, the next day I said to myself that there is no reason to give up. It is time to fight this and show everybody that God can bring you through hard times. I usually tell people who say why all the time to just stop saying it and say, "OK, I will take the task at hand and accomplish it, because God is with me." It even says in the Bible that Christians will go through hard times and face battles. This happens so we can come out of the battle a stronger person in God. Some people ask me, "Why did God do this to you?" I always say, "God did not do this! We live in an evil world and bad things happen to good people."*

The Number Thirty-One

As with Job: he lost everything. His family, finances, home, and friends. He refused to turn his back on God. He praised him; that's what I did. Like I always tell everybody, when something hits you don't cry about it. My best advice would be, Please, NEVER GIVE UP!!!!

Time and time again during Dustan's illness and especially during our grieving process 31 and 13 would show up in scripture right when we needed to feel loved or encouraged.

How fitting is each scripture for my boys.

Psalm 31, "I trust in you, O Lord."
Dustan had to completely put his trust in the Lord.

A Profession of Trust
To the chief Musician, A Psalm of David.
In thee, O Lord, do I put my trust;
let me never be ashamed:
deliver me in thy righteousness.
Bow down thine ear to me;
deliver me speedily:
be thou my strong rock,
for an house of defense to save me.
For thou art my rock and my fortress;
therefore for thy name's sake lead me,
and guide me.
Pull me out of the net that they
have laid privily for me:
for thou art my strength.
Into thine hand I commit my spirit:
thou hast redeemed me,

RESTING IN HIM

O LORD God of truth.I have hated them
that regard lying vanities;
but I trust in the Lord.
I will be glad and rejoice in thy mercy:
for thou hast considered my trouble;
thou hast known my soul in adversities;
and hast not shut me up into
the hand of the enemy:
thou hast set my feet in a large room.
Have mercy upon me, O LORD,
for I am in trouble:
mine eye is consumed with grief,
yea, my soul and my belly.
For my life is spent with grief,
and my years with sighing:
my strength faileth
because of mine iniquity,
and my bones are consumed.
I was a reproach among
all mine enemies,
but especially among my neighbors,
and a fear to mine acquaintance:
they that did see me without fled from me.
I am forgotten as a dead man
out of mind: I am like a broken vessel.
For I have heard the slander of many:
fear *was* on every side:
while they took counsel together against me,
they devised to take away my life.
But I trusted in thee, O LORD:
I said, Thou art my God.

The Number Thirty-One

My times are in thy hand:
deliver me from the hand of mine enemies,
and from them that persecute me.
Make thy face to shine upon thy servant:
save me for thy mercies' sake.
Let me not be ashamed, O Lord;
for I have called upon thee:
let the wicked be ashamed,
and let them be silent in the grave.
Let the lying lips be put to silence
which speak grievous things proudly
and contemptuously against the righteous.
Oh how great is thy goodness,
which thou hast laid up for them that fear thee;
which thou hast wrought for them
that trust in thee before the sons of men!
Thou shalt hide them in the secret of thy
presence from the pride of man:
thou shalt keep them secretly
in a pavilion from the strife of tongues.
Blessed be the Lord:
for he hath showed me
his marvelous kindness in a strong city.
For I said in my haste,
I am cut off from before thine eyes:
nevertheless thou heardest
the voice of my supplications
when I cried unto thee.
O love the Lord, all ye his saints:
for the Lord preserveth the faithful,
and plentifully rewardeth the proud doer.

RESTING IN HIM

> Be of good courage,
> and he shall strengthen your heart,
> all ye that hope in the LORD.

Psalm 13, "From Despair to Delight."
Dylan cried out to the Lord in his grief and went from despair to delight.

> *A Prayer for Help in Trouble*
> *To the chief Musician, A Psalm of David.*
> How long wilt thou forget me, O LORD?
> for ever? how long wilt thou hide thy face from me?
> How long shall I take counsel in my soul,
> having sorrow in my heart daily?
> how long shall mine enemy be exalted over me?
> Consider and hear me, O LORD my God:
> lighten mine eyes, lest I sleep the sleep of death;
> Lest mine enemy say,
> I have prevailed against him;
> and those that trouble me rejoice
> when I am moved.
> But I have trusted in thy mercy;
> my heart shall rejoice in thy salvation.
> I will sing unto the LORD,
> because he hath dealt bountifully with me.

After reading through Psalm 31 and Psalm 13 so many times, I could see that these were my sons' pleas. Their words may have been somewhat different but honestly not by much. Psalms are said to be poetry set to music. Both my boys loved music, Dustan playing instruments and Dylan writing poetry. The Psalms express worship. We are to praise God for who He is and for what He has done. Dylan now takes his creativity for words and his brother's love for music and puts

The Number Thirty-One

them in "spoken word" format. He is using his gifts and talents to give back from our tragedy.

Throughout our entire journey there has always been this special melody that played in my heart. It's my own special melody, using the all familiar words of the song, "It Is Well with My Soul." The first verse of this song goes like this:

> *When peace, like a river, attendeth my way,*
> *When sorrows like sea billows roll;*
> *Whatever my lot, Thou hast taught me to say,*
> *It is well, it is well with my soul.*

This song is written by Horatio Spafford in 1873 following a family tragedy in which his four daughters died aboard a ship that was struck by an iron vessel. This was the final in a series of tragedies; their son had died of scarlet fever three years prior, and afterwards the Great Fire of Chicago destroyed all their investments. His wife survived the shipwreck, and as his ship took him to meet her, he traveled the same path as his children had. Coming to the site of the shipwreck, he passed by where his daughters had gone down; he looked out above the waters and saw the giant waves. I am sure when the sea billows rolled it was if his grief had taken him over: images of his daughters being swept away in the darkness. He spent the hours after this experience writing the words of this hymn. *Whatever my lot, Thou hast taught me to say, It is well, it is well with my soul.*

I want to be really vulnerable here and say, Could I do that? I mean we had walked a really horrific, painstaking journey; but we had not lost everything. Some days it seemed that way. In reality, we still had a lot to be thankful for. Horatio Spafford had lost everything but his wife, and he could still pen the words, "Whatever my lot, It is well with my soul." When your grief and sorrow are so great you cannot even find the words to express it, nevertheless, it is well with my soul. I am often reminded of people who say, "I could never go through what you have

RESTING IN HIM

been through," and you know, you don't have to—not in your human strength. God gives us the grace to go through what we are going through at the time. You will get through it. It will be well with your soul. He will give you the peace that surpasses all understanding. You know what else He can give you? A ministry, a place where you can give back to others from what you have learned from your own misery.

Sometimes when we are walking in God's will we may think we are going in the wrong direction and we question ourselves. We must remember that God's path is not always the easiest. Even when we think we are going in the wrong direction GOD DOES HAVE A PLAN. I would much rather travel the rocky road with Him than the smooth road alone.

He has taught our family how to have joy in the journey no matter what the circumstances. I can honestly say that I am thankful for where I am. I'm not thankful that Dustan got cancer. What I am thankful for is all that we have learned on this journey. God continues to reassure our family that it is well within our soul.

The color red has always been Dustan's favorite color. When the boys were younger Dustan was always red and Dylan always blue. So red has always been significant to me. Red is the color of "the blood," which translates as the ultimate sacrifice of Jesus' blood for our sins. I see red and the number 31 every day. Is it because I am aware of them more now? All I know is that I see the color red differently. I see it as in comparison to the blood of Jesus, the ultimate sacrifice given for us all, and now I know Dustan lives forever. He precedes us, with so many others gone before us, as we await with great expectation what lies ahead, our forever home.

My perspective is so different now. I see my life here on earth as a brief journey to my real home. I am not supposed to be comfortable here. My heart always aches as if something is missing. Yes, I miss my son more than words can describe. But even more my heart knows that this is not where I belong. It longs for more; it longs for the completeness that only my Father can give.

God's word has become salve to our wounded hearts. These are some of our favorite scriptures:

1 John 3:1, "See what great love the Father has lavished on us, that we should be called children of God! And that is what we are! The reason the world does not know us is that it did not know him." (NIV)

Psalm 31:3, "Since you are my rock and my fortress, for the sake of your name lead and guide me." (NIV)

Jeremiah 31:3, "The Lord appeared to us in the past, saying: 'I have loved you with an everlasting love; I have drawn you with unfailing kindness.'" (NIV)

3 John 1:3, "It gave me great joy when some believers came and testified about your faithfulness to the truth, telling how you continue to walk in it." (NIV)

Ecclesiastes 3:1, "There is a time for everything, and a season for every activity under the heavens." (NIV)

Ecclesiastes 3:11, "He has made everything beautiful in its time. He has also set eternity in the human heart; yet no one can fathom what God has done from beginning to end." (NIV)

Colossians 3:1–3, "Since, then, you have been raised with Christ, set your hearts on things above, where Christ is seated at the right hand of God. Set your minds on things above, not on earthly things. For you died, and your life is now hidden with Christ in God." (NIV)

RESTING IN HIM

Proverbs 3:13, "Blessed are those who find wisdom, those who gain understanding…" (NIV)

Hebrews 3:13, "But encourage one another daily, as long as it is called 'Today,' so that none of you may be hardened by sin's deceitfulness." (NIV)

Psalm 133:1, "How good and pleasant it is when God's people live together in unity!" (NIV)

What do all these scriptures have in common? It's our story: love, trust, truth, guidance, wisdom, encouragement, eternity, seasons, beauty, and unity. Are these coincidences? Maybe you think so, but everything in life, down to the smallest of details, was designed by God himself. Nothing happens by accident.

Conclusion

Those who sow in tears
Shall reap in joy.
He who continually goes forth weeping,
Bearing seed for sowing,
Shall doubtless come again with rejoicing.
Bringing his sheaves with him.
(PSALM 125:5,6, NKJV)

I pray that as you have read every word in this book you have seen the goodness and glory of our Lord Jesus Christ. It is only through my weakness that His strength is seen. I wanted to write a book about our story, a mother and son's journey through cancer. Little did I know that God had a bigger plan. As I began writing "our" story it became God's story: where He was, and continues to be, in the midst of our everyday lives.

As Winston Churchill put it, "It is the end of the beginning." As this part of our journey ends a new beautiful one begins. Just as my sweet Dustan's life here on earth ended, his life really only just began. Ours too is just beginning.

RESTING IN HIM

As the above scripture states, those who sow in tears shall reap in joy. Our many years of tears have turned into JOY. There will always be a missing part in our hearts for Dustan. There will always be a scar from our grief. Now with joy we will let love seep from the broken places in our hearts, and our scars will be visible only for His glory.

Ecclesiastes 3:1 (31 ☺) states, "To everything there is a season, A time for every purpose under heaven" (NKJV). One of the reasons I love Tennessee is the beauty of each season: winter, spring, summer, and fall. I have to say that fall is my favorite. I love the beauty of all the vibrant colors, and to watch how the green changes to so many different colors. Isn't that just like us? We all seem to be the same, and yet when change occurs is when our true colors come forth.

Don't let change cause you to be dull and brittle. Just as the leaves fall from the trees, each in its own direction, learn to REST IN HIM so the vibrant color of His love shines forth as you float through the air with His beautiful light, reflecting His goodness.

As I look back over our season of grief I can see God's goodness and fingerprints throughout our journey. He was our constant companion. He led us every step of the way. I can see where every tear has turned into a gift. I am now a grief coach and can help others find their way through the darkness. I facilitate small groups where others can come together and be authentic and real with a community of believers. I am a better wife, mother, sister, daughter, friend—but mostly a better person, all because I let the broken places in my life become visible.

I wanted only good to come from my son's death. Ephesians 3:20,21 (NKJV), "Now to Him who is able to do exceedingly abundantly above all that we ask or think, according to the power that works in us, to Him be glory in the church by Christ Jesus to all generations, forever and ever. Amen." And Romans 8:28, "And we know that all things work together for good to them that love God, to them who are the called according to *his* purpose."

Conclusion

MY PRAYER:

Father,
Thank you that my story is mine; and because of the space between the dash (birth-death), I can live fully, knowing that you created me to live life abundantly. I have become your little handmaiden, Acceptance With JOY. Never will all things be as I choose, but I choose to Rest in You, knowing that you will walk alongside me on my journey. Each and every step I take in life can be a gift: not only for me, but as I own my story, others can see you and where you are in my story.

I lay all that I am at your feet. And I know that anything that rises up will be for the world to see you in my life. Amen.

MY PRAYER FOR YOU:

Father,
I pray for the person holding this book right now. I pray that their eyes will be open to who they really are in you, that they will have the courage to be real and authentic with not only themselves, but with those around them. For those who have been overcome with grief and tragedy, I pray you will give them renewed hope.

Father, may they see you in the midst of their pain, and be overwhelmed by your love. Let them know that their story can have a joyful outcome. With you all things are possible. Nothing is wasted in our lives. Jesus, you are not only in us; you are before us to lead, behind us to guard, beside us to support and comfort, and above to bless us. I pray that each person will know how much they are loved by you and so can trust in the plan that you have for their lives.

Father, thank you that we can own our stories and in return let others see you in the midst. Thank you that there is healing in speaking truth. Your word heals, restores, and redeems. I pray all this in your wonderful name. Amen.

RESTING IN HIM

To my precious firstborn:

I CAN ONLY IMAGINE—how beautiful the view you must see.

I CAN ONLY IMAGINE—how sweet the music must be.

I CAN ONLY IMAGINE—the love you must embrace.

I CAN ONLY IMAGINE—the smile that must be on your face.

I CAN ONLY IMAGINE—the day we will meet.

I CAN ONLY IMAGINE—as we run with excitement to greet.

I CAN ONLY IMAGINE—my Father and son hand in hand.

I CAN ONLY IMAGINE—how the water meets the sand.

I CAN ONLY IMAGINE—there is no beginning and end.

I CAN ONLY IMAGINE—until we are together again.

I CAN ONLY IMAGINE—but, oh, how I do.

I NEVER COULD IMAGINE—how much I would miss you.

I WILL DREAM ABOUT YOU—until we embrace again.

I WILL DREAM ABOUT YOU—until our new life begins.

31 Forever and Always.

MJCA basketball camp, June 2008

Bibliography

Chapter TWO
Concerning the Inner Life, Evelyn Underhill (Eugene, OR: Wipf & Stock Publishers, 2004).
"Strong," OED Online, Oxford University Press, 2018. en.oxforddictionaries.com/definition/us/strong.
"Normal," en.oxforddictionaries.com/definition/us/normal.
Catherine of Siena As Seen in Her Letters, Viva D. Scudder, trans. & ed., (New York: E.P. Dutton & Co., 1905).

Chapter THREE
"Trust," en.oxforddictionaries.com/definition/us/trust.
The Necessity of Prayer, E.M. Bounds (Radford, VA: Wilder Publications, 2008).
"Broken," Collins Dictionary, HarperCollins, 2018. collinsdictionary.com/dictionary/english/broken.
"Surrender," collinsdictionary.com/dictionary/english/surrender.
A Divine Invitation, Steve McVey (Eugene, OR: Harvest House Publishers, 2002).
Hinds' Feet in High Places: A Daily Devotional for Women, Hannah Hurnard and Darien B. Cooper (Shippensburg, PA: Destiny Image Publishers, 2013).

Chapter FOUR
"Experiencing God's Love," Billy Graham, *Billy Graham Evangelistic Association: Stories*, February 4, 2010. billygraham.org/story/billy-graham-on-experiencing-gods-love.
"Never Alone," *Undone*, Mercy Me (Writers: Bart Millard, Robby Shaffer, Pete Kipley, Nathan Cochran, Mike Scheuchzer, Barry E. Graul, Jim Bryson)

Chapter FIVE
"None Upon Earth I Desire Besides Thee," Rev. John Newton, 1779.

Chapter SIX
Jon Bon Jovi, "Top 25 Quotes by Jon Bon Jovi," A-Z Quotes, www.azquotes.com.
Discovering God's Purpose for Your Life, Beth Moore (Houston: Living Proof Ministries, 2007).
Oswald Chambers, Abandoned to God, David McCasland (Grand Rapids, MI: Discovery House Publishers, 2010).
"Buried Treasure," *Hinds' Feet*, Hurnard and Cooper.
Believing God, Beth Moore (Nashville: B&H Publishing Group, 2004).

Chapter SEVEN
"Obedient," Dictionary.com Unabridged, Random House, 2018. www.dictionary.com/browse/obedient.
"Faith," dictionary.com/browse/faith.
"Stand," dictionary.com/browse/stand.
"Bold," dictionary.com/browse/bold.

Chapter EIGHT
The Prayer That Changes Everything: The Hidden Power of Praising God, Stormie Omartian (Eugene, OR: Harvest, 2004).
Jesus Is Victor, Corrie ten Boom (Grand Rapids, MI: Revell, 1985).
The Gifts of Imperfection: Let Go of Who You Think You're Supposed to Be and Embrace Who You Are, Brené Brown (Center City, MN: Hazelden, 2010).
Paul: 90 Days on His Journey of Faith, Beth Moore (Nashville: B&H Publishing Group, 2010).
"The Adventure of Obedience," Glynnis Whitwer, *NIV, Real-Life Devotional Bible for Women: Insights for Everyday Life*, Lysa TerKeurst, ed. (Grand Rapids, MI: Zondervan, 2012).
Divine Invitation, McVey.

Chapter NINE
"Preparing for Life and Death," *5 Minutes a Day: His Devotional* (Nashville: Freeman-Smith, 2007).
"Just," en.oxforddictionaries.com/definition/just.
Hinds' Feet, Hurnard and Cooper.

Chapter TEN
"Grief," en.oxforddictionaries.com/definition/grief.
"Wave," dictionary.com/browse/wave.
"Ocean Waves: Energy, Movement, and the Coast," Amanda Briney, ThoughtCo.com, 2018. thoughtco.com/what-are-waves-1435368.
"Wednesdays With Beth," Beth Moore, featured on *LIFE Today With James and Betty Robison*. Lightsource.com/ministry/wednesdays-with-beth/series.
Lament for a Son, Nicholas Wolterstorff (Grand Rapids, MI: Eerdmans, 1987).
Out of Solitude: Three Meditations on the Christian Life, Henri Nouwen (Notre Dame, IN: Ave Maria Press, 1974).

Chapter ELEVEN
"Resolving Misunderstandings of the Exchanged Life," John Best, ThD, booklet self-published for his seminars (Dallas: Abundant Living Resources, April 1996).
The Normal Christian Life, Watchman Nee (Wheaton, IL: Tyndale House Publishers, 1977).
Divine Invitation, McVey.
Hinds' Feet, Hurnard and Cooper.
A Grief Observed, C.S. Lewis (New York: HarperCollins, 1994).
Gifts of Imperfection, Brené Brown.
Elisabeth Kübler-Ross, ekrfoundation.org.

Chapter TWELVE
The Girl's Still Got It: Take a Walk with Ruth and the God Who Rocked Her World, Liz Curtis Higgs (Colorado Springs, CO: Waterbrook Press, 2012).
Praying God's Word, Beth Moore (Nashville: BH Publishing Group, 2000).
Honor Yourself: An Offering for Those Lost in Dark Places, Terri St. Cloud (Accokeek, MD: Bone Sigh Arts, 2008).

Chapter THIRTEEN
"Never, Never, Never Give Up," *5 Minutes a Day*, Freeman-Smith.

CONCLUSION
"The End of the Beginning," Winston Churchill, speech at the Lord Mayor's Luncheon, November 10, 1942.

Eulogy ("Good Words")

Dustan left behind a legacy that cannot be defined by mere words. These are quotes from his teachers and friends.

"It seems ironic and fitting that God would send a young man to MJCA who from an earthly perspective came to the school to learn and be educated, but in God's eyes actually came there himself to teach and be an example for us all."

"Dustan did not just talk about faith, but he lived it out in his daily life."

"After a thirty-one month battle with leukemia, Dustan passed away from this life and received complete healing at the hands of his Lord and Savior, Jesus Christ. Through those years, he had taught our academy many valuable lessons that will never be forgotten. MJCA had joined Dustan and his family in this fight for life and gained a new respect for the character and willpower of Dustan, as well as an understanding of how to battle an incredible adversary with strength and integrity. Although we are glad that he will enjoy his pain-free eternal life, we will truly miss Dustan Gammon and all that he meant to MJCA."

"Dustan didn't want to be called a 'hero' and he didn't like any spotlight, but God has used Dustan to touch lives of people he never even met, and for years to come to touch lives of those who had the privilege of knowing him personally."

"You, my friend, are the true example of faith."

"Dustan, you were the bull's-eye on the target of life to shoot for. I love you and will forever miss you."

"Dustan, we will remember you always and forever. You have changed all of our lives and brought us closer together than anything could have."

"Dustan, we all love you and appreciate all of what you taught us."